Several years ago, we were treated to the fine book *10 Dead Guys You Should Know.* Its release beckoned for a companion volume, the equally fine book you now have in your hands. *10 Dead Gals You Should Know* features the most famous woman who ever lived—Mary, the mother of Jesus Christ—and the most famous woman martyr of all time—Perpetua. The book also opens up vistas into the lives and ministries of lesser-known women: for example, two Catherines—she of Siena, and Catherine Booth—and two Annes—Hutchinson and Dutton. Like the ten guys in the first book, these women were stellar examples of faithfulness, fearlessness, steadfastness, and fruitfulness. May you be challenged by their lives as their stories come alive for us today!

Gregg R. Allison

Professor of Christia   ...eology, The Southern Baptist

T0016898

Christians have needed this   ...   . book that tells the stories of some of the remarkable women in history that every Christian should know. Ciano and Maddock have done a brilliant job uncovering the stories of these women through the centuries: from the Bible and the ancient world, the Middle Ages and early modern periods, all the way up to the twentieth century. These women served God in a variety of extraordinary and costly ways. Among them were martyrs, missionaries, leaders of campaigns to end child prostitution, and then there was Corrie Ten Boom who hid Jews from the Nazis and then ran a rehabilitation centre for concentration camp survivors. Each chapter is both a compelling and moving story as well as a meticulously historically researched biography. This book is essential reading for Christians of all ages and backgrounds: women and men, girls and boys. You will be humbled, encouraged, and awe-struck by the courage and witness of these ten incredible women in Christian history.

Sarah Irving-Stonebraker
Associate Professor of History, Western Civilisation Program,
Australian Catholic University

Having read *10 Dead Guys You Should Know* and highly appreciating it, I had certain expectations about the companion book on the gals. I was not disappointed. As with the first book, this second one is well-researched and engagingly written. It is a gallery of ten women whose stories deserve to be widely known. Some of them I had no clue of. I benefited from the book not only because of its historical insights, but also for the many challenges that I received from encountering these women. Rachel Ciano and Ian Maddock have done a great job of combining fresh scholarship and spiritual wisdom.

Leonardo De Chirico
Pastor of Breccia di Roma church, Rome, Italy;
Lecturer in Historical Theology at Istituto di Formazione
Evangelica e Documentazione, Padova, Italy;
Director of the Reformanda Initiative

10 Dead Gals You Should Know is an innovative take on Christian history, one that focuses deliberately on unusual and challenging figures. These are women who were prominent and influential Christians in their religious communities from the ancient world to the twentieth century. Rachel Ciano and Ian Maddock have selected a brilliant and contrasting gallery of subjects, from Mary the mother of Jesus through Catherine of Siena, to Anne Hutchinson, and Gladys Aylward; every chapter reveals an individual powered by faith and determined to act upon it. The vivid and arresting language in which these women are described, and the solid scholarship of the authors, will guarantee a wide readership for the book.

Carole Cusack
Professor of Religious Studies, The University of Sydney

Rachel Ciano and Ian Maddock have produced an excellent book which supplies us with short biographies of important Christian women and which ought to inspire and encourage all of us to learn from the past in order to live in the present. *10 Dead Gals You Should Know* is the perfect complement to their previous *10 Dead Guys You Shoud Know,* because it is important for us to appreciate the wonderful significance of female agency in the building of the body of Christ. In recent decades, church historians have recognised the importance of the women in Church history, and it is a real blessing to see some of the harvest of this work made accessible through publications such as this. The Christian historian

Jaroslav Pelikan once wrote that "[b]y including the dead in the circle of discourse, we enrich the quality of the conversation." Well, with the historical, theological, and geographical terrain covered in Ten Dead Gals, Ciano and Maddock have certainly enriched our conversation about the blessing of women in God's church!

Mark Earngey
Head of Church History and Lecturer in Christian Thought
Moore Theological College

I thoroughly enjoyed reading *10 Dead Gals You Should Know: Leaving An Enduring Legacy.* This book is a well-researched, engagingly written, and insightful read that is sure to captivate readers and encourage them personally. As the subtitle suggests, the carefully curated stories of these ten women (who range from Mary the mother of Jesus, to twentieth-century missionary Gladys Aylward) mesh together to tell a bigger story. All ten have made a significant impact in the history of the church, and side by side, they illuminate some key moments in the unfolding story of Christian history. Maddock and Ciano pinpoint these moments and show readers how evangelical Christians have been unknowingly shaped by their contributions. I look forward to sharing this with my students and anyone who is interested in learning more about the history of Christianity.

Nicole Starling
Lecturer in Church History, Morling College

Fresh. Fascinating. Faith-building. From the first to the twentieth century, the women whose stories are recounted in this book – some famous, some less so – teach us about the cost of discipleship and the faithfulness of the Lord. But it is not just a chronicle of their lives: we learn about the theological debates that they engaged in, the social pressures they faced, and the ways their ministries have been interpreted. I was left hungry to hear more. May they serve as mentors to many!

Rhys Bezzant
Senior Lecturer,
Ridley College; Director of Johnathan Edwards Center,
Australia

The authors are right: you should really know about these 10 Dead Gals and what God has done in their extraordinary lives. Here is an impressive cloud of witnesses, from every era of church history, testifying to the power of the gospel to transform human beings. Ciano and Maddock retell these stories by combining good research with engaging writing.

Michael P Jensen
Rector, St Mark's Anglican Church Darling Point; Honorary
Research Associate, Sydney College of Divinity

I loved this book. I was inspired in my Christian walk and at times brought to tears. The authors have beautifully recounted the stories of women who in the Protestant tradition have often been neglected, to our loss. These women were exemplary disciples, courageous women who believed the gospel. They defied social conventions, some were abandoned, defamed, and persecuted but remained faithful. These women were writers, preachers, philanthropists, entrepreneurs, social activists, and evangelists. But most importantly, they were disciples of Jesus.

Ruth Lukabyo
Church History Lecturer at Youthworks College, Sydney.

10 DEAD ~~GUYS~~ GALS
YOU SHOULD KNOW

—

LEAVING AN ENDURING LEGACY

RACHEL CIANO
& IAN J. MADDOCK

CHRISTIAN
FOCUS

Scripture quotations marked 'NIV' are taken from the *Holy Bible, New International Version*®. NIV®. Copyright©1973, 1978, 1984 by International Bible Society. Used by permission of Zondervan. All rights reserved.

Paperback ISBN 978-1-5271-1041-0
ebook ISBN 978-1-5271-1074-8

Published in 2023 by
Christian Focus Publications Ltd,
Geanies House, Fearn, Ross-shire,
IV20 1TW, Great Britain.
www.christianfocus.com

Cover design by Peter Barnsley (HootSuite)

Printed and bound by Bell & Bain, Glasgow

Contents

Introduction
A Room (or Ten!) of Their Own

RACHEL CIANO & IAN MADDOCK

A cursory glance at the history of movie sequels suggests that not all spin-offs and follow-ups are automatically worth telling. Our hope is that this book proves to be an exception! After completing *10 Dead Guys You Should Know,* topping the list of most frequently asked questions was undoubtedly, 'when are you writing the companion volume – the one devoted to the lives of noteworthy Christian women?' *10 Dead Gals You Should Know* is the response to those perfectly reasonable questions. This was a project we felt compelled to undertake – to *not* write a sequel would be to leave our task half-finished.

In many ways, our aspirations for both collections are identical. If our assemblage of dead guys was intended to encourage *both* men and women in their faith, then our desire is that the 'gals' will do precisely the same. In other words, this isn't a book only *for* women – it's a book for everyone *about* women, whom God has used to accomplish His purposes in this world.

This literary portrait gallery is borne of two strong convictions: that history matters, and that women matter. 'Life includes a lot of empty space,' reflected Tom Crick, the narrator in Graham Swift's 1983 ode-to-the-relevance-of-history, *Waterland.* 'We are one-tenth living tissue, nine-tenths water; life is one–tenth Here and Now, nine-tenths a history lesson. For most of the time the Here and Now is neither now nor here.'[1] Crick's fictional character – a veteran history teacher who has just been made redundant after his beloved subject was summarily and poignantly cut from the curriculum – warned against succumbing to the cacophony of siren voices extolling the intrinsic irrelevance of the past in favour of a myopic focus on the present.

This collections of essays reflects our commitment, with Crick, to know and make known the realm of 'neither now nor here.' Christians have long understood the importance of history. Drinking from the deep well of the past inspires and equips us to critically engage – and empathise – with the world around us so we can live fruitfully on earth as citizens of heaven in the times and places God has determined for us.

We also believe that women matter. While many of their stories have been lost to history – or even remained untold – there is a great need to recover what we can.

---

1   Graham Swift, *Waterland* (London: Macmillan, 1992), 61.

That being said, this book isn't simply motivated by a desire to retrieve female voices for the sake of balancing the scales. In making both men and women in His image, God endowed men and women with equal value and honour. God sent His Son into the world to offer salvation to both men and women, and He gives His Spirit in equal measure to both men and women. In short, we're convinced that women matter because they matter to God. We believe women are integral, invaluable, worthy co-contributors in society and to God's plan and mission for the world.

In her famous 1929 essay 'A Room of One's Own,' Virginia Woolf describes the myriad of obstacles that have historically stood in the way of women's voices being heard. 'A woman must have money and a room of her own if she is to write fiction,' she wrote. To fiction we might well add theology or edifying Christian literature! Our desire is to furnish these very different women with ten rooms of their own, in order that we might profit from hearing their voices anew or afresh.

Collectively, these stories span two millennia and numerous continents: from Mary in first-century Judea, to Catherine Booth in nineteenth-century Britain, to Gladys Aylward in twentieth-century China. Some, like Catherine of Siena, rose from obscurity to exercise profound influence on high-stakes ecclesiastical wrangling in fourteenth-century Europe. Others, like Selina Hastings, the Countess of Huntingdon, used their inherited wealth and social prominence to advance the gospel across socio-economic boundaries. Perpetua and Jane Grey lived brief lives cut short by their conspicuous and brave fidelity to Jesus, while Corrie ten Boom, while no less courageous, lived a long life that testified to God's compassion and forgiveness. Some, like Anne Hutchinson, left England to make a new home in the infant colony of Massachusetts, only to be banished and ultimately die a lonely death as an outcast. Others, like Anne Dutton, had a ministry that was just as transatlantic in scope, even as she lived a predominantly sedentary life.

For all of their differences, every one of these women have left an indelible legacy on our collective, intergenerational Christian consciousness. Each is worth knowing in their own right; none were a 'plus-one' in a man's tale. 'Speed-dating' each of these 'dead gals' has been a joy for both of us. To know someone's story is a privilege; to have the opportunity to share it is even better. We hope you're encouraged in your Christian walk as you read of theirs.

Chapter 1: Mary

My Spirit Rejoices in God My Saviour

Rachel Ciano

The threat of scandal

A scandal is afoot – one that won't be easy to live down. It will be the talk of the town for years to come, a disgrace and an embarrassment of epic proportions that will set tongues wagging across the community. The appalling episode happens at a town party, and the incident has the potential to both shame the hosts and insult the guests. It's a local wedding, and the scandalous scene isn't a bad speech from a groomsman, mass food poisoning, or some dance floor disaster. Instead, the disgraceful humiliation is that they have run out of wine. The guests will think the host is lazy or irresponsible because he either can't provide what is needed for a party, or hasn't made the correct catering calculations. Even worse, they will think the host didn't care for them; love was to be shown in the sheer volume of party provisions. Everyone in town will remember this event if the unthinkable happens and news of the wine shortage gets out.

This party's invitation is dated around A.D 30, the location is probably in today's Lebanon, and the guest list included Jesus, His mum Mary, and His newly formed band of disciples. This party is not imaginary: these events really took place and are described in chapter 2 of John's Gospel. The host avoided the looming social disaster through a series of events kickstarted by Mary's simple yet loaded statement to Jesus: 'They have no more wine' (John 2:3 NIV). Clearly, Mary hoped to accomplish something by pointing this out. Jesus' response to her is even more laden with meaning: 'Why do you involve me? My hour has not yet come' (John 2:4 NIV), indicating that Jesus is not at the beck and call of His mother, but instead of His Father in heaven. In John's account of Jesus' life, 'the hour' is a significant term predominantly used to allude to His impending death on the cross, which will occur around three years after this wedding. Jesus weighed the significance of this moment, knowing it would begin a chain of events with only one ending.

Mary then stopped instructing Jesus and instead assumed the posture of a disciple, inviting the waiters to listen to Jesus, saying, 'Do whatever he tells you' (John 2:5 NIV). Jesus told them to fill six large stone water jars with water, around 600 litres in total. They obeyed without hesitating and to the utmost degree, filling them right up to the brim. Jesus then instructed them to take some to the master of ceremonies. Once the MC had tried it, he pulled the groom aside to compliment him on bringing out the best wine last, saying this generosity is unusual at a wedding. The cheaper wine usually comes out near the end when the guests are not in the best position to tell the difference! The party scene finishes with the ominous, marvellous words indicating the direction of Jesus' life – the cross: 'What Jesus did here in Cana of Galilee was the first of the signs through which he revealed his glory; and his disciples believed in him' (John 2:11 NIV). John is a book full of 'signs' and 'glory', paving the way to the last, definitive sign of Jesus' glory: His death and resurrection. This wedding marked a turning point in the course of history.

What can we make of Mary's role in this narrative? Understanding her in this story helps make sense of the rest of her. In the end, Mary must also learn what it is to be a disciple of Jesus. This story shows her moving from trying to influence Jesus and expecting Him to do something to address the wine shortage, to submitting to His timing, His 'hour,' and then pointing others towards listening to Him. At the end of this story, Mary is named in the group that travels with Jesus, alongside Jesus' earthly brothers and His disciples (John 2:12); she was enmeshed in the early community of Jesus' followers. If Mary were alive today, we could imagine her saying the same thing to us as to those waiters: 'Do whatever he tells you.' While it is not popular in current, Western culture to hear such calls to obedience, it is the person we listen to that makes the substantial difference. Mary is encouraging obedience to 'the Word [who] became flesh and made his dwelling among us,' the one who is 'from the Father, full of grace and truth' (John 1:14 NIV).[1] She is a picture of a woman who received grace from God her Saviour. Mary points us to her son and shows us a model of following Him – that is why she is a "dead gal" worth knowing.

The Mary of history
We are not told much about Mary in the Bible; the spotlight is rightly on her son, where Mary would want it to be. She is not out of sight in the narratives of Jesus' life, but she is certainly not centre stage. However, what we do encounter of her in the pages of Scripture is her testimony to God's kindness towards her, displayed in the living embodiment of God's grace and kindness: the Lord Jesus Christ, whom, humanly speaking, she brought into the world. The Gospels in the New Testament, especially Matthew and Luke, give us the greatest historical record of Mary, for, as they testify to Jesus' life, the thread of Mary's story also runs through them. The Gospels help us consider Mary's place in the world in her time, her pregnancy with Jesus and His birth, snippets of her life as a disciple of Jesus, and her witness to His death and resurrection.

---

1   'The Word became flesh and made his dwelling among us' is the only allusion to Jesus' birth in John's Gospel.

It is significant that Matthew's Gospel opens with the impressive genealogy of Jesus (Matt. 1:1–17). Jesus is in the family line of God's promises to Abraham, David, and their descendants. To Abraham, God promised to bring blessing to the whole world through his offspring. To David, God promised that one of his descendants would hold and rule God's kingdom forever – a kingdom shaped on the character of God Himself, full of mercy, justice, and enduring love (e.g. Gen. 12:1–3, 2 Sam. 7). Jesus' genealogy is full of scandal and what could be considered skeletons in the closet. Matthew, however, does not hide or airbrush over these scandals; rather, they are front and centre, forming the very opening of his Gospel. The presence of women in the genealogy is scandalous enough; however, added to this is that some are *Gentile* women, pointing to God's plan to bring salvation to the Gentiles too.

Furthermore, this honour roll includes women deemed dishonourable by many in that society, including prostitutes and outcasts. Tamar slept with her father-in-law, Rahab was the town prostitute, Ruth was a foreigner, and Bathsheba is only mentioned as another man's wife, brought into the Davidic family line through David's sin and his callous, cowardly murder of her husband. Mary appears as the final mother in this colourful genealogy – another curious, socially awkward mother. These women all point to God's grace and kindness that transforms social and religious stigmas, and that redeems and refashions lives: not just theirs, but also in the generations to follow.

Mary was an ordinary Jewish girl living in the first-century Roman Empire. As a result of her time and place in history, her life path was set out for her. She was engaged to marry Joseph, but before marriage or consummation, an angel tells Joseph and Mary separately that she will become supernaturally pregnant by the Holy Spirit. They are told to name the child Jesus, which means, 'The LORD saves' (see Matt. 1:18–25; Luke 1:26–38). This situation put Mary in a difficult position culturally: children born out of wedlock carried a stigma in her community and put her in grave danger too (cf. Deuteronomy 22:23). Mary's socially awkward situation is not from any insufficiency in herself. She is neither deserving of the unique position in history that God will place her in, nor of social shame that may come her way from a child born before she was married. Yet God's grace will work in these strange circumstances, as He did in the lives of the mothers in her family line. God's sovereign choice of Mary to bring the eternal Son into the world in human form is where the focus of Mary's life lies in these infancy narratives.

Luke contains the most about Mary out of the four Gospels. This is perhaps not surprising, for the Gospel of Luke particularly tells the tales of the down-and-outers of first-century Roman society, including women. Yet these outcasts enter God's kingdom because of their allegiance to the person and words of Jesus. In his two-volume narrative of Luke-Acts, Luke names Mary thirteen times and refers to her three more times. Luke depicts Mary as an active agent; Joseph often stands in relation to her, not the other way around. For example, he is *her* fiancé, he accompanies *her* to Bethlehem, he is named *after* Mary at the scene of Jesus' birth (see Luke 2:5, 16). Simeon addresses Mary rather than Joseph despite blessing both of them (Luke 2:33–34), and Mary speaks on behalf of her and Joseph (Luke 2:48).

Mary is identified as both 'favoured' and 'blessed' in Luke. Mary is told twice over via the angel Gabriel that she is 'favoured' (Luke 1:28, 30) as he comes to announce to her that she will 'conceive and give birth to a son...Jesus' (Luke 1:31 NIV). Mary is also called 'blessed' several times. Elizabeth, her cousin, proclaims it twice (Luke 1:42, 45), and Mary declares it of herself in her surging poetic praise of God and His grace in *The Magnificat* (Luke 1:48).[2] When a woman in the crowd calls out to Jesus, 'Blessed is the mother who gave you birth and nursed you'. Jesus replied, 'Blessed rather are those who hear the word of God and obey it' (Luke 11:27–28 NIV). Jesus emphasised 'rather' here, distancing Himself from allegiances to His earthly family and stressing the blessedness that comes from listening to and heeding God's words. However, Mary is also part of this blessed group that listens and heeds. After

---

2   *The Magnificat* comes from the Latin translation (the Vulgate), and is the first word of the poem, simply meaning 'magnifies', as in, 'my soul magnifies the Lord' (Luke 1:46).

asking Gabriel, 'how will this be,' echoing Zechariah's question of 'how can I be sure of this?' (Luke 1:18), she responds as a person of faith, taking God at His Word and believing He will bring about what He promises: 'I am the Lord's servant, may your word to me be fulfilled' (Luke 1:38 NIV). Mary is blessed and favoured by listening to God and believing the words He spoke to her, both as an individual and as part of the community that does likewise.

In this way, Luke's depiction of Mary is primarily as a disciple of Jesus, as an 'accessible exemplar' who demonstrates the life of not just a woman in the kingdom of God, but of all followers of Jesus.[3] Twice at the beginning of the Gospel, Luke draws our attention to Mary pondering the works of God. Mary 'treasured up all these things and pondered them in her heart' (Luke 2:19, 51 NIV). Luke also shows her embedded in the early church. In the last explicit mention of Mary in the New Testament, Luke names Mary as amongst the praying band of disciples in Jerusalem in the days following Jesus' resurrection (Acts 1:14). Luke portrays Mary as an 'everyday disciple' who is blessed by meditating on, heeding, and treasuring up in her heart God's words in God's community.

---

3   This term 'accessible exemplar' is borrowed from Joel Green, 'Blessed Is She Who Believed: Mary, Curious Exemplar in Luke's Narrative' in *Blessed One: Protestant Perspectives on Mary* ed. Beverly R. Gaventa and Cynthia L. Rigby (Louisville: Westminster John Knox, 2002), p. 10.

In Mark's Gospel, however, we see that Mary did not always fully understand the purposes of God. Mark helps us gain a portrait of Mary as sometimes perceiving and sometimes missing the point: sometimes listening and other times interfering and demanding (see, for example, Mark 3:21). In this way too, she is a disciple like us: *simul iustus et peccator,* which means 'at the same time justified and a sinner.' In Mark, she pleads for allegiance to blood relatives; Jesus took this opportunity to redefine family, highlighting that loyalty to Him created a new family (Mark 3:31–35). In fact, Jesus' family, including Mary, thought Jesus 'out of his mind' as he conducted some of His ministry (Mark 3:21), showing that at times Mary did not understand what her son was accomplishing in the world. Mary is also depicted in Mark as fearful, trembling, and bewildered at the mouth of the empty tomb, saying nothing to anyone, because she was afraid (Mark 16:8). Whatever we make of the abrupt ending of Mark, depicting scared disciples...including Mary...is a stark and honest finish, perhaps suggesting an invitation to the reader: 'how will you respond to the empty tomb?' The scene's honest portrayal of the disciples' reaction reeks of authenticity, and Mary is amongst the female cast members fearful on discovering that Jesus' body was not where they left it.

In terms of the incarnation, Mary as Jesus' mother demonstrates how utterly human the Son of God became. She helps point to the inescapable truth that Jesus was made like us in *every* way, yet was without sin

(Heb. 2:17, cf. 4:15). Just like us, Jesus existed as a minuscule embryo. Like us, when it was time to be born, He exited His mother's womb and had His umbilical cord cut. Like us, He relied on milk to sustain His tiny, vulnerable body, and He had His newborn head supported by His mother when He had no neck control. Jesus experienced complete human embodiment just as we do, and Mary was integral to this. She would have interacted with Him in the closest, physical ways as His human mother; she would have carried, kissed, cuddled, tickled, swaddled, washed, changed, fed, played with, and sung to her little baby. She would have helped Him navigate His way through toddlerhood, patiently teaching Him to make sounds, then words, and then sentences, and how to reach and grasp objects and use them. As He grew into boyhood, Luke tells us twice immediately after mentioning Mary that Jesus grew both physically and in wisdom (Luke 2:39–40, 51–52). In addition to taking care of His physical needs so that He 'grew and became strong' (Luke 2:40 NIV), Mary presumably also taught Him the Word of the Lord, how to memorise the Scriptures (as demonstrated in Jesus' constant quotation of them, particularly the Psalms), and taught Him how to pray. Perhaps she even taught Him how to cook (cf. John 21:1–14). As Mary bore, birthed, and breastfed Jesus, cared for Him as a growing boy, and prepared Him for adulthood, Mary proved integral to asserting and celebrating the complete humanity of the Son of God.

As Jesus grew into adulthood, Mary became one of His disciples. She remained close to Him, and we get glimpses of her in that band of early followers. Mary followed as Jesus headed, for the final time, to Jerusalem and His impending death. At the cross, Mary remained unto the last – a faithful, remnant disciple when others fled. Back when Mary and Joseph had taken newborn Jesus to the temple in Jerusalem, Simeon warned Mary; 'a sword will pierce your own soul too' (Luke 2:35 NIV). Now, that time had come. For a mother to watch her child die is to experience heartache of the acutest kind. She remained with her son, her precious firstborn whom she lived for and followed, as Roman soldiers...renowned for their brutality and skills in execution...worked their trade on Jesus and two other men with Him that Friday after the Passover celebration.

Yet in this grim and grisly scene, as Jesus pours out His life for the very ones inflicting this violence upon Him, Jesus continued to demonstrate His graciousness and love towards His disciples, including Mary. As Jesus hung there drawing in agonising, stunted breaths, He bequeathed to Mary a son in the form of His disciple, John. John had been one of Jesus' closest earthly companions; the previous night, he had sat affectionately close to Jesus as they celebrated the Passover meal, reappropriated as a meal of remembrance of what Jesus was now accomplishing. In this moment at the cross, John received a mum, and Mary received a son. Jesus' grace and kindness to her extended even in His dying breaths (John 19:25–27). Whilst Mary is one of the last to remain at the cross, she is among those first at the tomb. Three days later, Mary is part of a group of women who are the first witnesses of the resurrection of Jesus; death has been consumed in an instant by her son's ground-breaking, boulder-shifting resurrection. Jesus' permanent return from death is game-changing, and the world would never be the same again. Mary had front-row tickets to these remarkable events; her son was also God her Saviour (cf. Luke 1:47).

Mary *in* history

The Mary *of* history soon became the Mary *in* history. After her last appearance in the Bible amongst the community of Jesus' disciples (Acts 1:14) Mary's story and legend took on a very different path. Today, she is regarded by many millions of people as having a special place in the salvation of humankind, ultimately being a *co-redemptrix,* or co-redeemer, having participated with Jesus in redemption.[4] Among her other attributes and roles are some very illustrious titles indeed, including Mother of the Church, Queen of the universe, Mediatrix (because she mediates Jesus' grace having co-operated with God in accomplishing salvation), and Advocate (because she hears the prayers of God's people and

---

4   This fifth Marian dogma that Mary is 'co-redemptrix' has yet to be officially recognised, although it is widely believed and practiced throughout the Roman Catholic Church, including by the papacy. At the Vatican II Council (1962–65) Mary was given the titles of 'co-redemptrix' and 'mediatrix' but this is not yet an official teaching of the Roman Catholic Church.

advocates for them before her son).[5] She is believed to have been born free of original sin (Dogma of the Immaculate Conception, promulgated in 1854) and remained without sin throughout her earthly life, which is inextricably linked to the belief of her perpetual virginity. Deemed to be without sin, she is not subjected to the punishment for original sin, which is death, so she was assumed bodily into heaven as she neared death (Dogma of the Assumption of Mary, promulgated 1950).[6]

However, it is not simply the titles and attributes ascribed to her that point to how she is viewed; it is also how she is approached. She does not merely have the centre stage in salvation but is centre stage in many people's hearts. This is most evidently expressed in prayers to Mary. She is prayed to as the mother who has the ear of the Son (her son) and can therefore intercede on behalf of those who pray to her, for her unique position

---

5   These titles for Mary are evidenced, for example, in the Second Vatican Council Dogmatic Constitution on the Church, *Lumen Gentium* (1964), nn. 59-62. The full list of titles here attributed to Mary are 'Immaculate Virgin, Queen of the universe, Advocate, Auxiliatrix, Adjutrix, and Mediatrix.' See *The Documents of Vatican II*, ed. W.M. Abbott, S.J. (London-Dublin: Geoff rey Chapman, 1966). *Lumen Gentium* (The Light of the Nations) is also available via the Vatican website: https://www.vatican.va/archive/hist_councils/ii_vatican_council/documents/vat-ii_const_19641121_lumen-gentium_en.html

6   In the Roman Catholic Church, a dogma is a binding and unchanging belief revealed by God; it must be believed to be a faithful, communicant Catholic. See The Apostolic Constitution of Pope Pius XII, *Munificentissimus Deus* (Defining the Dogma of the Assumption), November 1, 1950. Available via the Vatican website. https://www.vatican.va/content/pius-xii/en/apost_constitutions/documents/hf_p-xii_apc_19501101_munificentissimus-deus.html

means she is more likely to be heard by God than they are. She is often viewed as the 'more approachable one,' the maternal figure to draw close to, while her son is more distant and removed. Mary is central to praying the Rosary, not only for the 'Hail Mary' prayers addressed to her, but the 'crowning' she is believed to receive every time the Rosary is completed.[7] Set prayers used in Marian devotion include the popularly used *Regina Coeli* (Queen of Heaven) and Hail Holy Queen. *Regina Coeli* draws attention to Mary's intercessory role:

Queen of Heaven, rejoice, alleluia.
For He whom you did merit to bear, alleluia.
Has risen, as He said, alleluia.
Pray for us to God, alleluia.
Rejoice and be glad, O Virgin Mary, alleluia.

For the Lord has truly risen, alleluia.
Let us pray.
O God, who has been pleased to gladden the world by the Resurrection of your Son our Lord Jesus Christ, grant, we pray, that through his Mother, the Virgin Mary, we may receive the joys of everlasting life.
Through the same Christ our Lord. Amen.

---

7   It is believed that Mary has revealed to a number of people that a rose is given to her each time a 'Hail Mary' is prayed, and a completed Rosary, which means 'crown of roses' gives her exactly this – a crown of roses. The rosary is therefore believed to be the most important of spiritual devotional practices. Leonardo De Chirico, *A Christian's Pocket Guide to Mary* (Fearn: Christian Focus, 2017), p. 55.

Physical spaces and places also testify to Mary's prominence in the devotional and spiritual practices of millions of people who hyper-venerate her.[8] Church buildings dedicated to Mary span the globe in their thousands, with one of the oldest and most important being Santa Maria Maggiore (St Mary Major) in Rome, which remains a centrepiece and model of Marian devotion. Upon his election in 2013, Pope Francis committed the world and his papacy to Mary.[9] The day after his election, he laid flowers at the foot of a statue of her at Santa Maria Maggiore, praying to her that she would protect Rome.[10] Smaller Mary shrines are scattered amongst everyday spaces like houses and gardens, schools and hospitals, all demonstrating her accessibility. There are also special places throughout the world where Mary is said to have appeared, and shrines have subsequently been built in her honour, which pilgrims can visit. One such place is Lourdes

8   The Council of Nicea (A.D. 787) established that saints were to be venerated *(dulia)* while Mary was to be hyper-venerated *(hyper-dulia)* De Chirico, *Mary*, p.33. In Catholic theology, supreme worship and adoration *(latria)* is reserved only for the Trinitarian Godhead.

9   "Pope Entrusts World to Immaculate Heart of Mary", *Catholic News Agency* online, October 13, 2013, https://www.catholicnewsagency.com/news/28237/pope-entrusts-world-to-immaculate-heart-of-mary

10 Upon his election on March 13, 2013, he indicated his plans for prayer to Mary for the following day. "Transcript: Pope Francis' First Speech As Pontiff", *NPR* online, March 13, 2013, https://www.npr.org/2013/03/13/174224173/transcript-pope-francis-firstspeech-as-pontiff

in the south of France, which is visited by as many as six million people annually. They approach the site of Mary's 'appearance' as humble pilgrims on their knees, seeking her mercy and healing for themselves or a loved one. Temporal spaces are also devoted to Mary; feast days are dedicated to her, with the month of May in the liturgical calendar focusing on Marian prayers and devotion.[11]

The Mary *of* history becomes the Mary *in* history

How did the Mary *of* history become this version of Mary *in* history? What follows is a very brief account of how this transformation took place.[12] While the early church recognised the four Gospels in the New Testament as a reliable record of the events surrounding Jesus' life, several other documents provide further details of the infancy narratives, as well as a lot more details of Mary's life. They place Mary, rather than Jesus, at the centre of the story, and she is cast as a heroine whose holiness uniquely positions her to be the agent through which the incarnation will take place. Rather than being a fellow-disciple amongst the community of Jesus' followers, she is cast as a leading character in the narrative, and thus brings salvation along with her son. Much is also made of her virginity, which is claimed to have been maintained

---

11 For further details, see De Chirico, Mary, pp. 60–2.

12 For further details on this, see De Chirico, *Mary,* pp. 19–52 and Gregg Allison, *40 Questions about Roman Catholicism* (Grand Rapids, MI: Kregel Academic, 2021) pp. 251–68.

after Jesus' birth, and miraculously, also through the birth process itself.[13] These documents include *The Protoevangelium of James,* (c. 2nd century A.D.) and the *Dormition of Mary,* (c. 2nd – 4th century A.D.). Whereas the New Testament Gospels were all composed in the same century that Jesus walked the earth, these texts are composed far too late to be reliable testimony, and the early church did not recognise them as worthy of being included in the canon of Scripture.

As the early church grew over the coming centuries, people sought to clarify, articulate and explain the relationship between God the Father, God the Son, and God the Holy Spirit, as well the nature of the Son in terms of the relationship between His humanity and divinity. At times, these debates went awry, and several Trinitarian and Christological controversies emerged. As the church sought to address these, a significant declaration was made that impacted the understanding of Mary. The Council of Nicea (A.D. 325) affirmed Jesus' complete humanity and divinity in response to Arius' and his followers' insistence that Jesus was not eternally God. However, far from being the end, Nicea proved something of the beginning, and the debate around the

---

13 This belief in Mary as 'perpetual virgin' is one of the four Marian dogmas and began from the fourth century onwards. The Council of Constantinople (A.D. 553) referred to Mary as *Aeiparthenos* ('ever-virgin'). The Church went beyond affirming her status as virgin *ante partum* (before birth) and started to refer to Mary as 'ever virgin' *post partum*, and even *in partu* (during the birth).

nature of Jesus raged on across the length and breadth of the Roman Empire. In A.D 431, Mary was officially proclaimed *Theotokos,* literally 'God-bearer', or 'mother of God' at the Council of Ephesus.[14] *Theotokos* was meant to declare the God-ness of Jesus, at the same time as upholding the unity of His person, against Nestorius whose teaching was thought to threaten this unity of His divinity and humanity. However, what began as a statement about Jesus was soon proclaimed as a statement about Mary. In the immediate aftermath of the Council of Ephesus, Pope Sixtus III built the church of Santa Maria Maggiore in her honour to celebrate this proclamation.[15]

When the bishop of Rome, Damasus, asked Jerome to translate the Bible into a unified Latin translation in A.D 382, Jerome set to work on the Vulgate, as in the 'vulgar' or common tongue, which in that time and place was Latin. Jerome was aware of the magnitude and weightiness of the task, writing to Pope Damasus in A.D 383:

> You urged me to revise the old Latin version, and, as it were, to sit in judgement on the copies of Scriptures... the labour is one of love, but at the same time both perilous and presumptuous...[W]hy not go back to

---

14 Jaroslav Pelikan helpfully defines *Theotokos* as 'the one who gave birth to the one who is God.' See Jaroslav Pelikan, *Mary Through the Centuries: Her Place in the History of Culture* (Yale: Yale University Press, 1996), p.55.

15 De Chirico, *Mary,* p.30.

the original Greek and correct the mistakes introduced by inaccurate translators…We must confess that as we have it in our language [i.e. Latin] it is marked by discrepancies, and now that the stream is distributed into different channels we must go back to the fountainhead [i.e. the Greek].[16]

Despite Jerome's best efforts to return to the original Greek manuscripts and produce a reliable Latin translation, several translation choices missed the mark and subsequently had huge theological repercussions. One such choice regards Luke's twice-over description of Mary as 'highly favoured,' as previously discussed (Luke 1:28, 30). The Vulgate translated κεχαριτωμενη (kecharitomene) as *gratia plena,* 'full of grace,' suggesting that grace was almost a substance which she was full of and which merited her role in salvation history; that her role as Jesus' mother was on account of her merit, rather than undeserved favour. Over time, Mary as 'full of grace' was understood as a title for Mary, and that she possessed an overflow of grace she could share with the faithful in their times of need. Erasmus, in the sixteenth century, an age that recovered and devoted their attentions to the original manuscripts and languages of the Bible, instead demonstrated that the Greek simply meant 'favoured one' or 'one who has found favour.' Nonetheless, by this

---

16 See Philip Schaff and Henry Wace, *The Nicene and Post-Nicene Fathers. Volume 6: St Jerome : Letters and Select Works, The Nicene and Post-Nicene Fathers. Second Series* (Grand Rapids, Mich.: William B. Eerdmans, 1979), pp. 487–88.

stage, Mary's place in possessing and being a conduit of God's grace was already cemented, and as the Latin Vulgate is still the official translation of the Roman Catholic Church, it would take a momentous shift for this conception of Mary to change.[17]

Mary, our woman of faith
The beliefs about Mary described above have not held a complete monopoly across history, and a significant shift started to occur in the Protestant Reformation of the sixteenth century. It was primarily a movement to recover biblical truths that many people in the church believed had been lost in the Middle Ages. Reformers sought to go back to what the Bible said about Jesus, particularly trying to answer the crucial question, 'what must one do to be saved?' The Roman Catholic Church in the sixteenth century was criticised for abandoning the Christian faith as spelled out in the New Testament, and these reformers sought a return to this historical faith. Reformer Martin Luther had a particularly soft spot for Mary and believed in her immaculate conception and her perpetual virginity; as the Mother of God, she had 'all honor, all blessedness, and her unique place in the whole of mankind, among which she has no

---

17 While Protestant churches don't have an official translation (although different churches do tend to highly favour one over another), the importance of the Hebrew and Greek versions is acknowledged by all evangelicals.

equal.'[18] He continued, 'men have crowded all her glory into a single word, calling her the Mother of God. No one can say anything greater of her or to her.'[19] Other reformers, however, were more tempered in her praise and objected to her hyper-veneration.[20] Over time in these Protestant churches, Mary largely disappeared. As new hymns were composed, she was markedly absent from those crafted to celebrate the birth of Jesus. Imagery of her was destroyed, and Protestants tended not to create images or paintings of her. If Protestants did make artworks depicting Mary, they contained very different thematic, stylistic and symbolic choices as a result of the marked departure from the Roman Catholic Church's representation of Mary.

This absence of Mary continues today in many Protestant contexts, thinking, and discussion, save her brief appearance around Christmas or Mother's Day.[21] Evangelical Christians seem to say less about Mary than the New Testament does, often treating her with 'cold neglect.'[22] This might be the case because evangelicals

18 Martin Luther, 'The Magnificat,' in *Luther's Works,* vol. 21, ed. Jaroslav Pelikan (St. Louis, MI: Concordia, 1956), 326.

19 Ibid.

20 For further details, see Timothy George, 'The Blessed Evangelical Mary', *Christianity Today* (December 2003). See footnote #8 for discussion of 'hyper-veneration.'

21 There have, however, been a number of attempts over the years to cast a more biblical portrayal of Mary, but this as yet has not made its way into mainstream evangelical conversations.

22 George, 'The Blessed Evangelical Mary', p. 36.

consider Mary has been 'claimed' by Roman Catholicism and are unsure what to do with her in their traditions. The Bible encourages us to have a realistic picture of Mary and we are in no way to hyper-venerate her because she was an ordinary person just like the rest of us. However, she is still a disciple to emulate, whose own faith encourages ours. Her faith brings blessings both to herself, as well as to people everywhere. As Elizabeth said to Mary, 'Blessed is she who has believed that the Lord would fulfil his promises to her!' (Luke 1:45 NIV). In this way, Mary models faith for us to copy. She is the 'accessible exemplar,' the 'ordinary disciple' who demonstrates that faith, at its core, is listening to and believing that God will keep His Word and fulfil what He has promised. For all Mary's ordinariness, doubts, and difficulties, what stands out about her is her trust in God and His unrelenting kindness, embodied and displayed for all to see in the person of Jesus whom, humanly speaking, she brought into the world. Mary was a disciple as well as His mother, and her status as the former trumps her status as the latter.

In refuting those who were cautious of honouring Mary lest she be put before Jesus, Alexander Stuart Walsh reflected:

> It was of Him she spoke when exclaiming: 'My soul rejoices in God my Saviour!' Can one truly honor Him and despise and ignore the woman who gave Him human birth?…She bore Him, then lived for Him.

She honored herself in bearing Him, and was His mother, His teacher, and His disciple. He revered her, she worshiped Him...believing in His divinity, she yet enjoyed the nearness to Him of a mother.[23]

We honour Mary by honouring her son. At the same time, we honour Mary by emulating her as a disciple of her son. Mary models hearing God's Word; she listens to Gabriel, and responds in obedience, despite the total disruption it will bring to her life plan. Mary models the close proximity to Jesus one of His followers will strive for: where He is, she is usually found. Mary models being a faithful member of the church, with the final recorded words about her life pointing to her meeting in fellowship and praying with fellow disciples; her spiritual family had become a bigger vision to her than her physical family. Finally, Mary models praise and celebration of the works of God.[24] Her most extended speech recorded is the crescendo of praise in the *Magnificat*, which is all about God and His wonderful works in her story and in the world's story: what He has done in the past, what He is doing, and what He will do. May we echo Mary's *magnum opus* in our praise of our mighty God.

---

23 Alexander Stewart Walsh, *Mary: Queen of the House of David and Mother of Jesus* (New York: H. S. Allen, 1886), pp. 555–6. Language updated for clarity.

24 These four areas of discipleship that Mary models for us are adapted from De Chirico, *Mary*, pp. 97–8.

My soul glorifies the Lord
and my spirit rejoices in God my Saviour,
for he has been mindful
of the humble state of his servant.
From now on all generations will call me blessed,
for the Mighty One has done great things for me—
holy is his name.
His mercy extends to those who fear him,
from generation to generation.
He has performed mighty deeds with his arm;
he has scattered those who are proud in their inmost
thoughts.
He has brought down rulers from their thrones
but has lifted up the humble.
He has filled the hungry with good things
but has sent the rich away empty.
He has helped his servant Israel,
remembering to be merciful
to Abraham and his descendants forever,
just as he promised our ancestors.

Luke 1:46b–55 (NIV)

For Further reading

Leonardo De Chirico, *A Christian's Pocket Guide to Mary* (Fearn: Christian Focus, 2017).

B.R. Gaventa, and C.L. Rigby (eds.), *Blessed One. Protestant Perspectives on Mary* (Louisville, KY: Westminster John Knox, 2002).

Chapter 2: Perpetua
Christians to the Lion!

RACHEL CIANO

A crime that deserved death

Five young people – Christian women and men – were eating breakfast within the gaol where they were held captive. They were residents of Carthage, in the North African section of the Roman Empire, and they had been recently arrested, all accused of the same serious crime. Four were arrested together; perhaps they had been followed to the location of their felony by someone keen to turn them over to the authorities. They were suddenly hauled to the local town centre during their meal, and news of their public appearance quickly spread around the neighbourhood. A crowd gathered to watch the scene unfold. They climbed the platform, which was made available so that the onlookers could hear their words. Four of them – some teenagers – were interrogated there in the prisoner's dock and publicly confessed to their crimes, knowing full well that they were liable to be sentenced to death.

Finally, the authorities came to the fifth prisoner, a twenty-two-year-old, respectable, well-born, married woman. She had a small infant son about to be used as a pawn in the spectacle. At that moment, her father appeared at her side with her young son, and, drawing her aside, begged her to 'have pity on your baby.'[1] The local governor, Hilarianus, also tried to persuade her to change her confession to avoid the death penalty. He appealed to her father and young son: 'Have pity on your father's grey head; have pity on your infant son.'[2] How could this young woman escape the fate that was before her? How could she ensure she was alive to care for her child? In the governor's words that day, all she needed to do was 'offer the sacrifice for the welfare of the emperors,' which in that day, was Roman Emperor Septimius Severus (A.D. 193–211).[3]

The crime these individuals confessed to that day was converting to Christianity. The guilty group included the young woman known to us as Vibia Perpetua, or Perpetua for short. Saturninus, Secundulus, and two slaves… Revocatus and Felicitas…were her fellow accused.[4] We

---

1   *The Passion of Saints Perpetua and Felicitas,* 6. In Patrick L. Geary (ed.), *Readings in Medieval History,* vol. 1 (Toronto: University of Toronto Press, 2010), p. 60.

2   Ibid.

3   Ibid.

4   *Passion,* 2. Geary, *Medieval History*, p. 58.

know Perpetua was 'of good family and upbringing' and was most likely a member of a high-ranking Roman family.[5] However, her social status was still not enough to protect her.

Upon that platform, after she refused to offer the sacrifice to the emperors that Governor Hilarianus requested of her, he went on: 'Are you a Christian?' She replied simply, 'Yes, I am.'[6] Clearly, this 'confession' was understood as deserving of death, for her father rushed to her side again and begged her to recant her faith. Her father knew her life was at stake in this admission. He tried so hard to save her that Hilarianus ordered him to be beaten for his efforts. Perpetua tells us that she felt sorry for her aging father, especially as she had just been beaten by the authorities in gaol herself. Her father now silenced, Hilarianus delivered the verdict: they were all condemned to die at the claws and paws of the wild beasts in the Roman arena.

The Passion of Saints Perpetua and Felicitas
We know of Perpetua and her story from *The Passion of Saints Perpetua and Felicitas*, which is mainly Perpetua's account of her arrest, trial, and visions in prison. It is a precious and rare piece of writing from a woman in this period, and perhaps the first Christian biography. The night before her execution, she handed over her writing to another Christian to finish the account of her life and

---

5   Ibid.
6   Passion, 6. Geary, *Medieval History*, p. 60.

death in the Roman arena. It was her 'passion' – her record of suffering and death – in the same way we speak of Jesus' 'passion.' Carthage (modern-day Tunis in Tunisia) was a hotbed for Christianity in the second century. Conceivably these arrests took place to try and squash the religion from booming. It is also where the famous Christian writer and apologist, Tertullian, lived.[7] Is it possible Tertullian compiled the final account of *The Passion,* providing the introduction and conclusion; it bears his style and interest areas.[8]

We know little of Perpetua's life before her arrest. We get glimpses, but it is not much. She was born around A.D. 181 (as she was about twenty-two when she died in A.D. 203). We know she was married, had a young son, and was from a family of good standing in the community. Felicitas, the other woman executed with Perpetua, seems to have been her servant girl, so Perpetua was of a particular class to warrant having help around the home. We also know her dad wasn't a Christian: a lot of the account of her trial and time in prison features his pleas for her to stop being so stubborn about her

7   The Greek word for 'apologist' *(apologia)* means speaking in defence, particularly of a position or action. As such, an apologist is someone who defends a position, not, as the term might suggest, apologises for it. In the second century, there was a category of Greek Christian writers who were termed 'apologists' such as Tertullian and Justin Martyr. They presented a defence of Christianity to outsiders and did so particularly in response to persecution.

8   Tertullian was a Montanist, and *The Passion of Saints Perpetua and Felicitas* has the hallmarks of this movement, including martyrdom, asceticism, and female prophesy.

faith. However, even though we only encounter her final days in *The Passion*, this narrow window into her life is a source of great encouragement towards courage in the face of severe adversity.

We were condemned to the beasts

That day in Carthage in early A.D. 203, when Perpetua admitted to her 'crime,' a death sentence wouldn't have been unexpected, nor the manner of her execution. She records that 'we were condemned to the beasts.'[9] Christians were often scapegoats in Roman society and ended up in the Roman arena. Tertullian wrote:

> If the Tiber rises as high as the city walls or if the Nile does not send its waters up over the fields, if the heavens give no rain, if there is an earthquake, if there is famine or pestilence, straight away the cry is, 'Away with the Christians to the lion!' What, shall you give so many to a single beast? Tell me, how many calamities were there before...the coming of Christ[10]

A dreadful death in the arena was not a new experience for Christians. They regularly made appearances in Roman blood sports and were condemned to 'fight' gladiators or wild beasts (the victims were unarmed and sometimes chained). It amounted to inhumane

---

9   *Passion*, 6. Geary, *Medieval History*, p. 60.

10 Tertullian, *Apology*, 40.2. For this translation, see Tony Lane (ed.), *The Lion Christian Classics Collection* (Oxford: Lion Hudson, 2004), p. 37.

execution for public entertainment. Emperors and local governors often held and funded these crowd-pleasing antics to garner the support of their constituents. They knew what the populace liked, and used their wealth in this grotesque way to demonstrate their generosity and benevolence. Tertullian was scathing in his condemnation in *De Spectaculis* ('On Public Shows'), arguing that gladiatorial games constituted murder.

Emperor Nero (A.D. 54–68) revelled in brutality towards Christians as early as the first century. After a fire swept through Rome, which conveniently cleared the way for his massive Golden Palace, the *Domus Aurea*, Nero arrested Christians to divert attention away from himself. The Roman historian, Tacitus, while not himself a Christian and severely disliking them, nevertheless offered a sympathetic description of their fate:

> To suppress this rumour [that Nero had instigated the fire], Nero fabricated scapegoats – and punished with every refinement the notoriously depraved Christians (as they were popularly called)...Their deaths were made farcical. Dressed in wild animals' skins, they were torn to pieces by dogs, or crucified, or made into torches to be ignited after dark as substitutes for daylight. Nero provided his Gardens for the spectacle, and exhibited displays in the Circus [i.e., the arena].[11]

---

11 Tacitus, Annals, xv.43. See Michael Grant (trans.) Tacitus on Imperial Rome (Harmondsworth: Penguin, 1956), A.D. 354. Tacitus continued: 'Despite their guilt as Christians, and the ruthless punishment it deserved, the victims were pitied. For it was felt that

Up until A.D. 313, when Emperor Constantine the Great issued the Edict of Milan, which decreed that Christianity be tolerated, various waves of persecution occurred against Christians. The severity and extent of these attacks usually depended on the particular policy of the Roman Emperor in charge. Until A.D. 250, persecution of Christians was primarily localised and erratic. From A.D. 250 onwards, persecution became empire-wide and systematised; Emperors such as Decius and Diocletian made it their policy to find and kill Christians unless they renounced their faith. Five decades after Perpetua's death, Decius issued an edict in A.D. 250 requiring everyone to obtain a certificate to prove that they had made the required sacrifices to the Roman gods and emperor. However, at the time of Perpetua's arrest, the persecution of Christians was still in this first phase, typified by the religious policies of Emperor Trajan (A.D. 98–117). Trajan's policies directly impacted Perpetua and her friends' fate, so it is worth pausing to think about the legacy he delivered to the emperor of Perpetua's day – Septimius Severus.[12]

---

they were being sacrificed to one man's brutality rather than to the national interest.'

12 Before Trajan was Emperor, he had sacked Jerusalem in A.D. 70 and carried off articles from the Temple. Trajan's Arch in the Roman Forum has sculptural reliefs depicting temple articles being carried off by Roman soldiers.

Perpetua's predicament: Trajan and Septimius Severus

We get to see Trajan's policy on Christians in the Roman Empire in the correspondence between himself and the Roman Governor of Bithynia, Pliny the Younger. Governor Pliny wanted Emperor Trajan's advice on how to, legally speaking, handle Christians. Pliny was concerned that 'the contagion of this superstition has spread not only in cities, but in the villages and rural districts as well' and that 'persons of all ages and classes and of both sexes' were appearing before him on the dangerous charge of being a Christian.[13]

Pliny interrogated Christians but found 'nothing but a depraved and extravagant superstition' where people met together, recited a hymn 'to Christ, as to a god,' and bound themselves by oath not to commit theft, robbery, or adultery, before finally eating together.[14] Nevertheless, Pliny wanted direction and possibly affirmation from Emperor Trajan. So he outlined for him his approach to the situation: if a Christian appeared before him and recanted, that is, offered sacrifices to the Emperor and 'did reverence, with incense and wine, to your image,' 'worshipped your image,' and 'cursed Christ, a thing

---

13   Henry Bettenson and Chris Maunder (eds.) *Documents of the Christian Church* (Oxford: Oxford University Press, 1999), p. 4.

14   Ibid. Pliny's letter is a wonderful window into early Christian practices, even if viewed suspiciously by society. For example, these 'oaths' may well have been viewed in a conspiratorial light by Roman society.

which, it is said, genuine Christians cannot be induced to do,' Pliny let them go.[15] Trajan replied:

> You have taken the right line, my dear Pliny, in examining the cases of those denounced to you as Christians...they are not to be sought out; if they are informed against, and the charge is proved, they are to be punished, with this reservation – that if anyone denies that he is a Christian, and actually proves it, that is, by worshipping our gods, he shall be pardoned as a result of his recantation.[16]

That is, if people appeared before the authorities accused of being Christians, they should be punished. However, if they denied being a Christian and proved it by making an offering that the authorities knew 'genuine Christians cannot be induced to do,' they would be let go. The governor's request to Perpetua and the others that day to 'offer the sacrifice for the welfare of the emperors', and the lengthy legal process (they spent a long time in prison) demonstrates that the authorities were probably hoping that she and the others would recant their position and be pardoned.

Christians responded in different ways when faced with persecution. When confronted by the authorities, some gave in and performed the required sacrifices or oaths, or publicly renounced their faith in Jesus. Sometimes giving in to the authorities meant handing

---

15 Ibid., pp. 3–4.
16 Ibid., p. 5.

over Christian texts to be burnt. Sometimes it also meant ratting out your neighbours. However, for others, they could not bend. In the words of Pliny to Trajan, they were executed for stubbornness: 'obstinacy and unbending perversity deserve to be punished.'[17]

In A.D. 202, Emperor Severus added to Trajan's policy, resulting in Perpetua's arrest. Severus faced a fair few challenges, which appear to have led him to issue this edict. He had become Roman Emperor in A.D. 193 primarily through military might. The fact that Severus owed his position to military accomplishments rather than clear dynastic succession meant there was always the danger that a military uprising might topple him. He had put an end to civil wars that threatened the empire, but the threat of a new outbreak was only around the corner. On top of this, the Roman Empire was constantly under threat from 'barbarian' tribes, people who lived beyond the empire's borders, mainly east of the Rhine and Danube rivers.

For the first few years of Severus' reign, there were relatively low levels of persecution for Christians in the empire. After that, however, the difficulties he faced in trying to keep a very socially, geographically, and religiously diverse empire united drove him to attempt to bring the empire together through an official policy

---

17 J. Stevenson, *A New Eusebius: Documents Illustrating the History of the Church to AD 337,* 2nd ed. (revised W. H. C. Frend, London: SPCK, 1987), p. 18.

of syncretism.[18] All religions and philosophies were tolerated as long as they worshipped under the banner *Sol invictus*, the Unconquered Sun, who reigned above all. As part of this, the A.D. 202 edict also outlawed conversion to Christianity or Judaism under penalty of death. Irenaeus was one early, notable casualty of this landmark imperial edict. Origen's father also suffered the same fate in Alexandria around this time (Alexandria was also in Roman North Africa). Clement, too, had to flee Alexandria to seek refuge in more obscure parts of the empire.

Severus' edict seems to be why Perpetua and her fellow Christians were targeted – they had recently converted to Christianity. They were 'young catechumens,' which meant they were preparing for baptism.[19] As part of this preparation, Christians in the second century – and in many centuries since – received instruction on what it meant to be a Christian. Perpetua was baptised during her imprisonment – that's how new to the faith she was. That is also perhaps why four of them were arrested together: is possible they were apprehended as they went together to a preparation class. During her imprisonment, other Christians visited her to attend to her needs (gaols at this time required visitors to feed and clothe prisoners) and they brought her child, demonstrating that Severus' issue was *converting* to Christianity – this deserved death. Her

---

18 Syncretism means a mixing or blending of religious and philosophical systems.

19 *Passion,* 2. Geary, *Medieval History,* p. 58.

visitors were not apprehended, but could freely come and go, presumably because they had been Christians for a while (two, Tertius and Pomponius, are referred to as deacons in the church). The importance of community and connection, especially in hardship, is demonstrated here; these visitors cared for and, in a sense, suffered alongside Perpetua in her ordeal.

Offer the sacrifice for the welfare of the emperor
Twice in her trial, Perpetua tells us that she was asked by the governor to 'perform the sacrifice' and 'offer the sacrifice for the welfare of the emperor', which she refused to do.[20] Why could she and the others not perform this necessary and fundamental civic act? Why their stubborn refusal? All she needed to do was perhaps pour out a drink offering and call Caesar, 'Lord.' That was their 'get out of gaol free' card. However, for Perpetua, and every Christian before and since, bearing the name 'Christ' means they cannot call another by this name. In their minds, there is one Lord, who was not and could never be Caesar, or any ruler on earth. For this reason, Roman society viewed Christians with suspicion – as seditious, treasonous, and dangerous citizens.

Roman society also viewed Christians as just plain ridiculous. Cartoon graffiti from this period depicting Christians still survives today. These etchings on walls include images of Christians worshipping a donkey on a cross. Christians were ludicrous for claiming to follow

---

20   *Passion*, 6. Geary, *Medieval History*, p. 60.

such a man – they might as well be honouring a braying donkey for all the good it would do them.

Christians were at odds with the Roman religious landscape. Overall, Roman religion was a flexible system. There was a plethora of gods and goddesses, the big twelve inherited from the twelve ancient gods of the Greeks. The Romans took over the gods of the Greeks – Zeus became Jupiter, Artemis became Diana, and so on. Then, as the Roman Empire expanded across present-day Europe, North Africa, and the Middle East, they picked up and incorporated the religious systems of the people they conquered. Roman religion was a visible religion: there were shrines, statues, and temples everywhere you looked. Private homes and public spaces were littered with signs of Roman religious life – roads, markets, homes, and even the army bore the images of the gods. Early Christians were called 'atheists' – you couldn't see their god, and their 'temples' bore no images of Him!

Roman religion was pliable, syncretistic, polytheistic and able to absorb new gods and religious practices. However, there was one thing that Roman religion had no flexibility for: refusing Caesar as Lord and not performing sacrifices in his honour. Failing this test of allegiance is one of the main reasons Christians were executed in these early centuries. Before Perpetua, Jason (first century) and Polycarp (second century) had similarly refused to swear by 'the genius of Caesar' (an oath of allegiance to the emperor as a god).[21] Jason and other Christians were dragged from his house to answer city officials on the charge that 'they are all defying Caesar's decrees, saying that there is another king, one called Jesus' (Acts 17:6–7 NIV). Polycarp, bishop of Smyrna (modern-day Turkey), was executed in a stadium around A.D. 155 after refusing the proconsul's request to 'Swear by the genius of Caesar,' 'Repent,' Say "Away with the atheists!"...'Swear, and I will release you; curse the Christ.' Polycarp calmly replied, 'Eighty-six years I have served him, and he has done me no wrong; how then can I blaspheme my king who saved me?'[22] The Roman state could not tolerate Christians' stubbornness on this issue.

Caesar is more ours than yours
Allegiance to the emperor was a complex issue for Christians. Tertullian addressed this issue when he wrote his famous *Apology* in Carthage during Septimius Severus' reign, around A.D. 197. Since Perpetua was in Carthage at the same time, she may have read it before her death five years later. He addressed it particularly to the magistrates in Carthage but also to Roman provincial governors in general. Although written before the edict

---

21 The *Genius Caesaris* was an oath invented under Julius Caesar (see *Dio Cassius,* xliv. 6). During Caesar Augustus' reign, certain days were dedicated to the worship of the genius of the emperor, a practice that only grew under subsequent emperors. See Bettenson and Maunder, *Documents,* 11.

22 'The Martyrdom of Polycarp,' ibid.

of A.D. 202 banning conversion to Christianity, Tertullian still addressed the persecution Christians faced, trying to demonstrate how absurd it was. He summarised the issue: '"You do not worship the gods," you say; "and you do not offer sacrifices for the emperors."...So we are accused of sacrilege and treason. This is the chief ground of charge against us—nay, it is the sum-total of our offending.'[23]

In his *Apology*, Tertullian denied Christians were disloyal to the emperor, by arguing that in fact, Christians pray for the emperor, and that, in the end, 'Caesar is more ours than yours':

> We are ever making intercession for all the emperors. We pray for them long life, a secure rule, a safe home, brave armies, a faithful senate, an honest people, a quiet world — and everything for which a man and a Caesar can pray...But you say, we merely flatter the Emperor; and we feign the prayers we utter, to evade persecution...Examine God's words, our scriptures... know from them that a superfluity of benevolence is enjoined on us [i.e. we are required to show extreme kindness], even so far as to pray to God for our enemies and to entreat blessings for our persecutors... But why need I say more of the religious awe, the piety, of Christians, where the Emperor is concerned? We must needs respect him as the chosen of our Lord. So I have a right to say, Caesar is more ours than yours, appointed as he is by our God.[24]

---

23 Tertullian, *Apology*, 10.
24 Tertullian, *Apology* 30.4–5; 31; 33.1

The day of their victory dawned

Following their trial and condemnation, Perpetua and her fellow prisoners were kept in gaol until their execution. The day before they were to die, they were given one last feast, at the taxpayers' expense. They turned it into a 'love feast' – a Christian meal commemorating Jesus' death and resurrection.[25] Perhaps they recalled Jesus' words the night before His own execution when He instituted this widely-practised commemorative meal: 'If the world hates you, keep in mind that it hated me first…if they persecuted me, they will persecute you also' (John 15:18–25 NIV). Tomorrow came. *The Passion* records that 'the day of their victory dawned, and they marched from the prison to the amphitheatre joyfully as though they were going to heaven, with calm faces, trembling, if at all, with joy rather than fear. Perpetua went along with shining countenance and calm step…putting down everyone's stare by her own intense gaze.'[26]

Perpetua's servant, Felicitas, had just given birth in prison and therefore was able to enter the arena along with them (pregnant women couldn't be executed). So she went 'from one bloodbath to another, from the midwife to the gladiator.'[27] When they got to the amphitheatre gates, they were told to put on the robes of priests: priests of Saturn for the men, priestesses of Ceres

---

25   *Passion*, 17. Geary, *Medieval History*, p. 63.

26   *Passion*, 18. Ibid.

27   Ibid.

for the women. They told their captors that they would happily give their lives but would not do this. Even in their last moments, they wanted to maintain their loyalty to Jesus by not submitting to Roman religious practices.

Authorities brought them into the arena as they were, and Perpetua began singing a psalm. As the condemned men passed by Governor Hilarianus, they motioned and gestured to say, 'you have condemned us, but God will condemn you.'[28] The crowd called for them to be scourged by a line of gladiators, and they rejoiced in sharing in the same sufferings of Jesus. The Roman amphitheatre was a menagerie of creative cruelty, and animals featured heavily in the arena. Two of the men, Saturninus and Revocatus, were set before a leopard and afterwards put in stocks and attacked by a bear. Another man, Saturnus, was tied to a wild boar and dragged along; however, the boar fatally gored the gladiator who tied him on, whereas Saturnus survived.[29] They chained Saturnus up for the bear to tear at him, but the bear seemed to have stage fright and wouldn't come out of the cage.

The women fared little better. At first, Perpetua and Felicitas were tied up in nets naked for a mad bull to attack.[30] However, even the crowd was horrified by

---

28 Ibid.

29 Saturnus had not been arrested with the others, but had voluntarily presented himself before the governor and pronounced that he had converted to Christianity.

30 In Greek mythology, the god Zeus transformed himself into a bull to try and seduce, or rape (the terms are similar) a young woman

this treatment of two young women, one of whom had clearly just given birth ('the milk still dripping from her breasts').[31] Perpetua and Felicitas were removed from the nets and given loose tunics to wear. Then, Perpetua was tossed by the bull, falling heavily on her back and tearing her tunic. At this, her hair came loose, so she asked for a pin to put it back up with – disordered, loose hair on women was a sign of mourning, and she wanted this to be her 'hour of triumph.'[32] She went over and helped Felicitas to her feet, for she had been crushed on the ground, and the two stood side by side.

The gruesome spectacle was nearing finishing time, so the prisoners walked (one was carried unconscious) to the usual spot where gladiators would slit the condemned people's throats and end the show. However, the crowd demanded they all be executed in front of them, so they 'got up and went to the spot of their own accord as the people wanted them to, and kissing one another they sealed their martyrdom with the ritual kiss of peace.'[33] Saturnus was the first to be dispatched. The rest died quietly and without moving, except Perpetua, who 'took the trembling hand of the young gladiator and guided it to her throat' when his first attempt excruciatingly failed.[34]

---

called Europa. Some historians suggest that the practice of tying up naked women in the arena for a bull to attack was designed to emulate Zeus' actions.

31 *Passion*, 20. Geary, *Medieval History*, p. 64.

32 Ibid.

33 *Passion*, 21. Geary, *Medieval History*, p. 64.

34 Ibid.

For the consolation of the church

In the epilogue to *The Passion of Saints Perpetua and Felicitas*, the author writes that for those who worship Jesus, reading accounts such as this are 'consolation', and 'bear witness to one and the same Spirit who still operates, and to God the Father almighty, to his Son Jesus Christ our Lord, to whom is splendour and immeasurable power for all the ages.'[35] As those living in a very different time and place from Perpetua, what consolations, or encouragements, might we draw from her example?

First, this showdown about who can rightly be called 'Lord' is nothing less than what Jesus faced. The Romans executed Jesus, for He had the gall to claim that He, not Caesar, was Lord. For Jesus to call Himself 'Christ' – meaning 'anointed one' or 'king' – was death-deserving blasphemy to the Jewish people of His day, and death-deserving treason to the Romans. Jesus' trial and death are laden with references to His kingship: from Governor Pilate's questioning, 'Are you the king of the Jews?' (John 18:33 NIV), to the dark, mocking irony of the soldiers, 'Hail, king of the Jews!' (John 19:3 NIV), who made him a kingly, thorny crown and dressed him in 'royal' robes. Later, as Pilate continued trying to set Jesus free, the Jewish leaders summed it up perfectly: 'If you let this man go, you are no friend of Caesar. Anyone who claims to be a king opposes Caesar'

---

35 Ibid.

(John 19:12 NIV). 'Shall I crucify your king?' Pilate asked them. 'We have no king but Caesar,' the chief priests replied, at which Pilate handed Jesus over to be killed (John 19:15 NIV). Even the notice that hung above Jesus' head on the cross told of His dreadful crime: 'This is the King of the Jews.' It appeared in not one but three languages: Aramaic, Latin and Greek. Everyone needed to know His blasphemy and treason.[36]

Perpetua and her friends were therefore in good company, as are all those who suffer for their allegiance to Jesus when it puts them at odds with allegiance to rulers in this world. Jesus and the New Testament writers continually testified that persecution for belonging to the spiritual family of Jesus was to be expected (see, for example, Mark 8:34–35). The book of Acts is full of the persecution of first-generation Christians. Peter, in between his escape from prison around A.D. 44, and his death in Rome under Emperor Nero two decades later (c. A.D. 64), considered his response to hostility in this world.[37] He wrote to encourage scattered, persecuted Christians to position their hearts and lives well, in the face of hardship. These Christians knew the world was hostile to them – they were living that reality. Into that

---

36 Aramaic for the local Jewish population, Latin for the Romans, and Greek for everyone. Greek was still the most spoken language in the Roman Empire at that time, a hangover from when Alexander the Great ruled these parts, not the Romans, and why the writers of the New Testament wrote in this language.

37 According to an early historian, Eusebius, Peter asked to be crucified upside down, so as not to die in the same way as his beloved Jesus.

space, Peter wrote, quoting Isaiah, 'Do not fear their threats; do not be frightened', before setting out how Christians were to conduct themselves in the face of opposition: 'but in your hearts revere Christ as Lord. Always be prepared to give an answer to everyone who asks you to give the reason for the hope that you have. But do this with gentleness and respect, keeping a clear conscience' (see 1 Peter 3:13–17 NIV). He continued, 'if you suffer as a Christian, do not be ashamed, but praise God that you bear that name' (see 1 Peter 4:16 NIV).

Perpetua was probably familiar with warnings and encouragements such as these and even the normalising of severe persecution for following Jesus. Perhaps it formed part of her classes in preparation for baptism. We can imagine these sorts of words in her mind as she stood on that platform refusing to renounce Jesus, and later in gaol and in the arena. Perpetua's experience is not entirely unlike the experience of other followers of Jesus. Many early disciples met their death for refusing to deny they had seen the resurrected Jesus. Today, many Christians are killed each year worldwide for continuing to testify and believe the same.

Like Perpetua, many Christians can identify with the pressure that family members place on them to renounce their faith. At one point, Perpetua asked her father whether the object in front of them – a water jug – could be known as anything else. When he replied, 'No,' she responded, '"Well, so too I cannot be called anything other than what I am, a Christian." At this, my father was so angered by the word "Christian" that he moved towards me as though he would pluck my eyes out. But he left it at that and departed.'[38] She is gracious and firm in her answer to her father, following Peter's encouragement to Christians under pressure for their faith.

Two centuries later, also in North Africa, Athanasius would point to scenes like Perpetua's death as one proof of the resurrection of Jesus:

> A very strong proof of this destruction of death and its conquest by the cross is supplied by a present fact, namely this. All the disciples of Christ despise death; they take the offensive against it and, instead of fearing it, by the sign of the cross and by faith in Christ trample on it as on something dead...death is no longer terrible, but all those who believe in Christ tread it underfoot as nothing, and prefer to die rather than to deny their faith in Christ, knowing full well that when they die they do not perish, but live indeed, and become incorruptible through the resurrection... for men who, before they believe in Christ, think death horrible and are afraid of it, once they are converted despise it so completely that they go eagerly to meet it, and themselves become witnesses of the Saviour's resurrection from it.[39]

The trouble that comes from allegiance to Jesus, and the joy of following Him, are our reality, too. This account of

---

38 *Passion,* 2. Geary, *Medieval History,* p. 58.

39 Athanasius, *On the Incarnation,* 5:27.

Perpetua's trial and death does serve as a 'consolation,' because it bears witness to the same God that Perpetua and her friends put their trust in, and the hope of the resurrection to come.

For further reading

The Passion of Saints Perpetua and Felicitas in Patrick L. Geary (ed.), *Readings in Medieval History*, vol. 1 (Toronto: University of Toronto Press, 2010).

Joyce E. Salisbury, *Perpetua's Passion: The Death and Memory of a Young Roman Woman* (London: Routledge, 1997).

Chapter 3: Catherine of Siena Bride of Christ

IAN MADDOCK

'My dear babbo, I hope you will not love yourself selfishly; nor your neighbors selfishly, nor God selfishly,' she wrote:

> I want you to be the sort of true and good shepherd who, had you a hundred thousand lives, would be ready to give them all for God's honor and other people's salvation... Let us concentrate no longer on friends or relatives or on our own material needs, but only on virtue and promotion of spiritual matters.

The 'daddy' receiving this unsolicited correspondence – in Italian, 'babbo' was a colloquial term of endearment for one's father – was Pope Gregory XI. The letter, a mixture of religious fan mail, audacious reprimand, and inspirational pep talk, couldn't have come from a less likely source in fourteenth-century Europe – a twenty-something, semi-literate Italian woman named Catherine Benincasa: Catherine of Siena.

Her purpose in writing with such familial directness? Coaxing the pontiff to relocate the papacy from Avignon (in modern day France) back to its historical home in Rome:

> Pursue and finish with true holy zeal what you have begun by holy intent – I mean your return [to Rome] … Delay no longer… for your delaying has already been the cause of a lot of trouble… Up, father! No more irresponsibility! … Courage! Courage! Come, come to reassure God's poor servants, your children.[1]

Remarkably, he did come. Catherine succeeded in doing what nobody had been able to accomplish in the previous sixty years and in 1377 the Pope returned to Rome.

But over and above any geographic reforms such as these, Catherine's highest longing was the spiritual transformation of a church riven by corruption. As a female lay associate within the Order of Preachers, also known as the Dominicans (named after its early thirteenth-century founder, the Spanish priest Dominic de Guzmán), she was renowned as a 'mystic and an extreme ascetic, a prophet and a healer, an ambassador

---

1   S. Noffke (ed.), *The Letters of Catherine of Siena*. 4 Volumes (Tempe, AZ: Center for Medieval and Renaissance Studies, 2000-2008), 1:246-249.

for the pope and a tireless worker for church reform.'[2] She was an especially prolific correspondent (over 380 of the letters she dictated survive), variously exhorting and rebuking men and women from all segments of medieval society: cardinals, monks, nuns, hermits, family members, widows, soldiers, queens, prostitutes, poets – and yes, even Popes!

But what Catherine lacked in formal authority within her society or church, she more than made up for in God-given charisma that attracted a wide range of followers. Throughout her short life (she has been likened to 'a brief shooting star streaking across the sky'[3]), Catherine's reputation for personal holiness, wisdom – not to mention her powers of persuasion – extended far and wide: 'No tongue or pen could ever adequately describe the ... sweetness of her holy company; only those who were ever with her can have any idea of it,' wrote her mentor and earliest biographer, the future Master General of the Dominican Order, Raymond of Capua. Her devotion towards Jesus and longing to grow in love towards God and neighbour was from all accounts infectious: '[T]hose who heard her were so strongly drawn to good and took such delight in God that every trace of unhappiness disappeared from their hearts.'[4]

---

2   S. Fanning, *Mystics of the Christian Tradition* (Abingdon: Routledge, 2002), p. 128.

3   Fanning, *Mystics,* p. 128.

4   Raymond of Capua, *The Life of St. Catherine of Siena* (Charlotte, NC: Tan Books, 2003), p. 8.

Catherine's life trajectory was especially unusual given that, by inclination, she seems to have far preferred solitude over sociability, seclusion over society. It begs the question: how did this one-time recluse end up foregoing a life devoted exclusively to contemplation, prayer and religious introspection in favour of a highly visible – and controversial – public ministry?

His eternal benediction

Catherine was born on 25 March 1347 in Siena, Italy, the twenty-third child of Giacomo and Lapa Benincasa. Her father was a wealthy Sienese textile dye producer, while for the previous two decades her mother's life 'was an almost unbroken cycle of pregnancy and childbirth'; many of Catherine's siblings had died in infancy, including her twin sister Giovanna.[5] From all accounts, Catherine was a happy child. Her nickname was 'Euphrosyne', which means 'joy' in Greek, and also, in a sign of things to come, is the name of a fifth-century saint 'who turned her back on marriage so that she could give herself completely to Jesus in a kind of spiritual marriage.'[6]

Having survived a bubonic plague pandemic that swept through Europe between 1348 and 1350 – one third of her fellow townsfolk did not – in 1354 Catherine experienced a vision of the risen Jesus that set the tone

---

5 T. Undset, *Catherine of Siena* (San Francisco: Ignatius, 2009), p. 6.
6 J. Tyson, *Faith, Doubt, and Courage in 15 Great People of Faith: and What We Can Learn from Them* (Eugene, OR: Wipf and Stock, 2013), p. 66.

for the rest of her life. In his biography of Catherine, published in 1395, Raymond of Capua recounted how:

> hanging in the air in front of her eyes over the roof of the church of the Friars Preachers, she saw a most beautiful bridal chamber decked out in regal splendour, in which, on the imperial throne, dressed in pontifical attire and with the tiara on His head (that is to say, the monarchical papal mitre), sat the Lord Jesus Christ, the Saviour of the world.

Visible only to Catherine, Jesus – accompanied by the Apostles Peter, Paul, and John – looked:

> straight at her with eyes full of majesty, and smiling most lovingly, He raised His right hand over her, made the sign of the cross of salvation like a priest, and graciously gave her His eternal benediction. The grace of this gift was so immediately effective upon the little girl that she was taken right out of herself.[7]

Following Catherine's mystical experience – the first of many to come – she made a vow of virginity and began to devote herself to prayer and meditation. But by the time she reached her teenage years, her desire for a celibate life clashed with her parents' hopes that she would soon get married – hopefully to a wealthy husband who would help secure the family's flagging financial fortunes.

---

7   Raymond, *Catherine*, p. 9.

Catherine was having none of it. At first she fasted in protest. Then she cut off her long hair to make herself less attractive to a potential suitor – her father and mother had in mind the wealthy widower of Catherine's older sister. Her 'parents responded to her rebellion by forcing her to live a sort of 'Cinderella' life – doing the dishes, cleaning, and performing other household chores that were usually assigned to servants.'[8] But when she contracted a bout of pox at age seventeen – and defiantly refused any treatment – the matter was settled. Left 'disfigured, physically undesirable and hence unmarriageable,' she was now free to pursue a life of single-minded (and single) service towards God and His people.[9]

The longed-for habit
But having successfully thwarted her parents' best efforts to marry her off to 'some mortal, corruptible man,' Catherine now turned her attention to perpetually safeguarding her virginity. The institutional answer lay close at hand: the Dominican basilica (or church) and its Order of Preaching Friars in the centre of town. 'Day and night she turned untiringly to the Lord, imploring Him to grant this wish of hers': that she might join the Sisters of Penance of St. Dominic (later known as the

---

8   Tyson, *Faith, Doubt and Courage*, pp. 66-67.

9   F.L. Cross and E.A. Livingstone (eds.), 'Catherine, St., of Siena,' in *Oxford Dictionary of the Christian Church* (Oxford: OUP, 2005), pp. 304-305.

Dominican Third Order), often referred to in Siena as the Mantellate.[10]

The problem was, she didn't meet the usual selection criteria. The Mantellate were middle-aged widows, and Catherine was neither of these! But emboldened by a dream in which she saw Dominic himself welcome her as a Sister of Penance ('Sweetest daughter, take courage and fear no obstacle, for you will undoubtedly put on this habit, as is your wish'), she hoped her extreme asceticism – denying the needs of her body as a way of expressing her devotion to Jesus – would persuade them to bend the admission rules.[11]

While her religious zeal and longing for an intimate spiritual relationship with her Saviour was undoubtedly sincere, she was also motivated by a theology that was dangerously misguided. Her automatic (and unhelpful) categorisation of physical matter as intrinsically tainted and inferior compared to pure spiritual matter sadly translated into years of self-harm – and eventually her premature death as a 'divine anorexic.' Catherine wasn't a 'one-off' either. In fact, her attempts to accelerate mystical visions of Jesus through self-denial were quite common among women during the Medieval period (others who followed a similar regime included Margery Kempe and Angela of Foligno).

Catherine's parents had, by this stage, relented and allowed her 'to live in solitude and silence in her room,

---

10 Raymond, *Catherine*, pp. 30-31.
11 Ibid., p. 31.

going out for Mass at San Domenico (the Dominican Basilica).'[12] In her small monastic bedroom she set about reviving 'the ancient deeds of the holy Fathers of Egypt,' especially their desire to grow closer to Jesus through self-denial and visualising His crucifixion. In her desire to mimic Christ's suffering, Catherine barely ate or drank: 'the mere smell of [food] used to make her feel sick.' She barely slept either, training herself to subsist on 'no more than half an hour every other day… and only gave in to it when exhaustion forced her to.'[13] When she did sleep, it too was an opportunity for self-mortification: 'She joined a few boards together and that was her bed. She sat on these boards to meditate, she remained prostrate on them to pray, and when it was time to go to bed she stretched herself out on them, dressed, to sleep.' Speaking of clothing, this too was an opportunity for self-discipline: 'For a time she wore a hair shirt,' but later exchanged it for 'an iron chain, which she wound so tightly around her waist that it sank into her flesh and almost chafed the skin away.'[14] Other times she used a chain to scourge herself. Just as Jesus had bled for her sins, she sought to imitate His self-sacrifice: in her own words, 'blood for blood.'[15]

---

12 S. Noffke, (ed.), *Catherine of Siena: The Dialogue* (New York: Paulist Press, 1980), p. 4.

13 Raymond, *Catherine,* pp. 34-35, p. 37.

14 Ibid., pp. 36-37.

15 Ibid., p. 38.

Eventually, her 'penitential zeal' was rewarded (by the Dominicans at least) and, at the age of eighteen, she received 'the longed-for habit.'[16] Finally, Catherine had secured 'an end to all this stupid insistence on marriage,' wrote Raymond. From now on 'she would be allowed to serve her true Bridegroom as she wished.'[17]

There! I marry you to me in faith

If the Bible describes the church as a collective bride, with Jesus as her bridegroom, then Catherine understood Him to be her very own mystical husband. Raymond's biography is full of Catherine's spiritual encounters with her Lord, but arguably none were more momentous (and graphic!) than her mystical wedding day. As the season of Lent approached in 1368, Raymond recounts how Jesus spoke to her, saying, 'Since for love of me you have forsaken vanities and despised the pleasure of the flesh and fastened all the delights of your heart on me... I have determined to celebrate the wedding feast of your soul and to espouse you to me in faith.'[18]

This was the marriage Catherine had been saving herself for! Those in attendance included a veritable 'who's who' of Biblical luminaries. As King David played 'sweet strains on the harp,' and Paul and John looked on as witnesses, the virgin Mary took Catherine by the hand and 'presenting her to her Son courteously asked Him to

---

16 Ibid., p. 43.
17 Ibid.
18 Ibid., p. 81.

marry her to Himself in faith.' Raymond continued, 'The Son of God, graciously agreeing,' placed a ring on her finger saying: 'There! I marry you to me in faith.'[19]

While Raymond described the wedding ring – visible only to Catherine – in lavish, though conventional, terms as being made of gold set with four diamonds, it's likely he sanitised the content of her actual vision so as to render it more palatable for public consumption. After all, in a number of her subsequent letters, Catherine often described her wedding ring as being made of a unique substance: not silver, gold, or even platinum – but Jesus' foreskin! For instance, to one nun she wrote,

> You see very well that you are a bride and that he has espoused you – you and everyone else – and not with a ring of silver but with a ring of his own flesh. Look at the tender little child who on the eighth day, when he was circumcised, gave up just so much flesh as to make a tiny circlet of a ring![20]

From the seclusion of her cell to public life
Not long after her spiritual wedding, Catherine's life took a turn for the public. Once more, the catalyst for her decisions came via a mystical experience with her Saviour-Spouse. Raymond relates how in her vision Jesus woke His bride 'from her sleep on the bed of contemplation,' and proceeded to call 'her from rest to labour, from silence to noise, from the seclusion of

---

19 Ibid., p. 82.
20 Noffke, *Letters*, 2:184.

her cell to public life.'[21] The mission that He had for her consisted of 'opening': 'Open, by ministering to them, the doors of souls, that I may enter into them. Clear the way for my sheep, that they may come and graze freely.'[22]

At first, Catherine admitted that she baulked at the prospect of entering the fray of a society battered by waves of plague, famine, and continual friction between feuding Italian republics: 'she felt such a pain in her heart that it seemed as though it was about to break.' Her greatest fear it seems wasn't the prospect of learning how to make small talk again, but instead a concern that the more she interacted with others, the less relational energy she would have left over for Jesus. But rather than viewing this new outward-looking phase of life as a relational zero-sum game, Jesus reassured Catherine that the more she actively loved others, her love for Him would actually increase: 'I have no intention of cutting you off from me; on the contrary, I wish to bind you more closely to myself, by means of love of the neighbour. You know that the precepts of love are two: love of me and love of the neighbour... You must walk, in fact, with both feet, not one, and with two wings fly to heaven.'[23]

Thoroughly persuaded, Catherine threw herself with gusto into 'works of charity... of two kinds,' categorised as 'corporal works of charity' and those 'for the good of

---

21 Raymond, *Catherine*, pp. 87-88.

22 Ibid., p. 88.

23 Ibid., p. 89-90.

souls.'[24] Not surprisingly, there was nothing half-hearted about her service: 'The charity infused into the heart of this holy maiden was such that ... she [was] almost continuously aiding her neighbours.'[25] As a member of the Mantellate, these good works typically entailed 'tending to the needs of the poor and sick' and 'nursing patients in hospitals and in their homes.'[26]

In the midst of this gritty urban ministry, there was plenty of opportunity for often stomach-churning acts of self-mortification. For instance, Catherine took it upon herself to care for a fellow Sister of Penance named Andrea, who had 'fallen ill with what the doctors called a cancer of the breast.' The infection 'had gone on eating away the flesh… until practically the whole breast was affected.' Lacking any medical means of preventing the disease from spreading, the 'horrible sore' produced 'such a frightful stench' that 'no one would help the poor woman or even go and see her.'[27]

No one, that is, except Catherine. After removing Andrea's bandages one day, 'thanks to the Devil rather than nature, she was assailed by a stench so unbearable that her inside turned over and a great sensation of nausea convulsed her stomach.' Determined to overcome

---

24 Ibid., p. 98.

25 Ibid., p. 108.

26 C. Cameron, *Leadership as a Call to Service: The lives and works of Teresa of Ávila, Catherine of Siena and Thérèse of Lisieux* (Ballan, VIC: Connor Court, 2012), 134.

27 Raymond, *Catherine*, p. 121.

her body's completely natural physiological reactions, she 'roused herself to holy anger against her own body… collected into a bowl the fetid stuff that had been used to wash the sore, along with all the pus, and, going away a little, gulped it all down.'[28] The culinary culmination of this dubious triumph of mind (or spirit) over matter came when she whispered to Raymond: 'Never in my life have I tasted any food and drink sweeter or more exquisite.'[29] Reflecting on incidents like this, Cameron's assessment that 'the health of [Catherine's] soul seemed to take precedence over the health of her body' seems like a gross understatement – pun intended![30]

Anderson notes that, 'While we may be inclined to agree with those who saw [Catherine's] eating habits as a sign of delusion, many people in the fourteenth century believed that it was only by the power of God's grace that she could drink pus.'[31] In fact, this was a rare recorded instance of Catherine eating much of anything at all. Faith-driven – though nonetheless pathological – 'holy anorexia' and bulimia seems to have been a constant feature of her life. But rather than being viewed as a genuine disorder that needed immediate treatment, her minimalist eating habits were celebrated and encouraged by those in her inner circle.

---

28 Ibid., p. 127.

29 Ibid.

30 Cameron, *Leadership*, p. 140.

31 C. Anderson, *The Great Catholic Reformers: From Gregory the Great to Dorothy Day* (Mahwah, NJ: Paulist Press, 2007), p. 104.

Today, we have very different understandings and approaches to eating disorders than in the medieval period. However, for sufferers of the illness, it is often a life-long, complex struggle. Nevertheless, God enables people to create healthy relationships with their bodies and with food. Lest we be tempted to follow Catherine's unhealthy body-spirit dualism, instead God offers us an integrated approach that celebrates both. Our bodies matter to God – He made them after all. 'Spiritual practices' that denigrate the value of the physical body are dualistic at best, and dangerous at worst.

Because Catherine often vomited anything that she ate – conspicuously aside from the bread and wine she consumed daily when she partook of the Lord's Supper – 'she was promoted by the Dominican friars as a woman who lived solely on the Eucharist.'[32] Indeed, like many of her thirteenth and fourteenth century mystic contemporaries, imbibing the bread and wine was a favourite way of catapulting Catherine into intense mystical experiences of union with Jesus. Afterwards she often went into a trance-like ecstatic state for three or four hours at a time, 'with her entire body becoming so rigid that she was immovable.'[33] Raymond even recounts instances of her levitating! 'In these ecstasies, in which the holy virgin became rapt like another Mary Magdalene, her body was sometimes raised up off the

---

32 Anderson, *Catholic Reformers,* p. 104.
33 Fanning, *Mystics,* p. 130.

ground along with her spirit, and it was quite evident that a great power was attracting her spirit.'[34]

I received His Head into My Hands

In addition to her ministry to the sick, the hungry and the dying, Catherine made the most of every opportunity to verbally proclaim the gospel. Whereas a century earlier Francis of Assisi is reputed to have said, 'preach the gospel, and where necessary use words,' Catherine was committed to a ministry of both word and deed. Indeed, if her works were, in effect, an eloquent non-verbal testimony to the gospel, she recognised that her motivations for pursuing these acts of service needed to be explained: they were a response to God's unmerited grace.

Jesus' sacrifice on behalf of – and in the place of – sinners was the cornerstone of the gospel Catherine shared. In one of her letters she wrote, 'The bond of payment for human sins was written on nothing less than lambskin, the skin of the spotless Lamb. He inscribed us on himself and then tore up the lambskin! So let our souls find strength in knowing that the parchment our bond was written on has been torn up.'[35] In another letter she urged a nun, 'Bathe in the blood of Christ crucified. See that you don't look for or want anything

---

34 Raymond, *Catherine,* p. 95.

35 Noffke, *Letters,* 1:65.

but the crucified, as a true bride ransomed by the blood of Christ crucified – for that is my wish.'[36]

On other occasions Catherine emphasised the way God longs to give us a new spiritual heart. For instance, in *The Dialogue* (which she referred to as 'my book') – an edited transcription, completed in 1378, of a mystical conversation held with Jesus during an extended trance – she likens Jesus to a bridge that enables sinners, 'to be drawn to union with [God].' The act of gazing at Jesus' heart is spiritually transformative:

> My Son's nailed feet are a stair by which you can climb to his side, where you will see revealed his inmost heart. For when the soul has climbed up on the feet of affections and looked with her mind's eye into my Son's opened heart in his consummate and unspeakable love… [t]hen the soul, seeing how tremendously she is loved, is herself filled to overflowing with love.[37]

Catherine even reportedly experienced, in bodily form, the dual biblical motifs of union with Christ and God's desire to 'create a clean heart' within us. After praying with 'utmost fervour' for this renewal using the language of Psalm 51, Jesus appeared to Catherine, 'opened her left side, took out her heart, and then went away.' A few days later he reappeared, placed his own heart inside her saying, 'I am giving you mine, so that you can go

---

36 Ibid., 2:184.

37 S. Noffke, *Catherine of Siena: The Dialogue*, Classics of Western Spirituality (New York: Paulist Press, 1980), pp. 26-28.

on living with it forever', before proceeding to close 'the opening he had made in her side.'[38] Raymond concluded his account of Catherine's spiritual cardiological surgery by reporting that 'as a sign of the miracle a scar remained on the flesh on that part of her flesh, as I and others were told by her companions who saw it.'[39]

Comforting people at the extremities of their lives (often in the midst of grief, starvation, mortal disease – even impending execution) was a constant feature of Catherine's ministry. One famous example took place in June 1375, when a political dissident named Niccolo di Toldo was sentenced to death. Hearing that he wasn't yet a believer, she quickly went to offer – and di Toldo accepted – the hope of the gospel in the face of his imminent beheading. His story 'could easily have remained a confused blur among the many who died at the executioner's hands' in fourteenth-century Italy, writes Prosperi. And yet, 'he was destined to become an unforgettable case, an inspiration for centuries to those who worked to provide Christian aid to the condemned.'[40]

Fearing dying alone, Catherine promised to remain with di Toldo to the very end. She even seems to have experienced some 'execution envy' too: three years later

---

38 Raymond, *Catherine*, p. 144-145.

39 Ibid., p. 145.

40 A. Prosperi, *Crime and Forgiveness: Christianizing Execution in Medieval Europe* (Cambridge, MA: Harvard University Press, 2020), p. 87

she reportedly wept tears of frustration when martyrdom eluded her during a mob riot in Florence, as she said '[God] did not fulfil my desire to give my life for Christ's dear bride'[41]. After waiting 'for him at the place of execution... in continual prayer,' di Toldo arrived and 'knelt down very meekly.' Catherine was more than simply present at his death: she 'placed his neck [on the block] and bent down and reminded him of the blood of the Lamb. His mouth said nothing but "Gesu!" (that is, Jesus) and "Caterina!"' These were his final words. She recalled that seconds later – 'I received his head into my hands.'[42]

Babylonian Captivity, Great Schism
By the early 1370s, Catherine had become something of a Sienese religious celebrity: 'Mamma' to an inner group of followers known as her *Famiglia* (or family). 'I have at times seen an endless stream of men and women coming down from the mountains and country towns around Siena, as though summoned by an invisible trumpet to see or hear [her],' reflected Raymond. 'I have seen them all stung with remorse not only by her words but at the mere sight of her and crying and sobbing over their own sins.'[43] Supernatural visions continued to punctuate her life. She experienced a 'mystical death,' glimpsing scenes from heaven and hell that served to

---

41 Noffke, *Letters,* 3:149

42 Ibid., 1:86-88.

43 Raymond, *Catherine,* p. 193.

renew the urgency of her evangelism. In April 1375, while in Pisa, she experienced the 'stigmata': nail marks in her hands, visible to her alone, reminiscent of Jesus' passion.

During the last decade of her life, Catherine was 'drawn into the turbulent world of Italian politics and attempted to mediate the incessant disputes among the independent city-states of her native Tuscany.'[44] By now a long way from the hermit-like existence she had once lived, Catherine also found herself at the centre of dramatic geopolitical struggles, helping to broker a peace deal between the city of Florence and the Avignon-based papacy. Perhaps most famously, in 1377, she even convinced Gregory XI to return to Rome, thereby ending the so-called 'Babylonian captivity' of the church – a period of 'exile' that had lasted seven successive popes and nearly seventy years.

Catherine was clearly unafraid to speak truth-to-papal-power. Gregory XI seems to have found her bluntness variously refreshing and annoying, but ultimately persuasive. Propelled by visions of Jesus chastising a corrupt church, and following the qualified permission to rebuke ecclesiastical authorities granted by Thomas Aquinas a century earlier ('It must be observed... that if the faith were endangered, a subject ought to reprove his or her prelate even publicly'[45]), Catherine wrote letter after letter urging for the reform of the church.

44 Fanning, *Mystics*, p. 131.
45 Thomas Aquinas, *Summa Theologiae*, 2.2.33.4

'I heard that you have appointed some cardinals. I believe it would be to God's honor and better for you to be careful always to choose virtuous men. Otherwise it will be a great insult to God and disastrous to holy Church,' she wrote to her spiritual 'babbo' in December 1375. Blending encouragement and prophetic warning, she continued, 'And then let's not be surprised if God send us his chastening sources, and justly. I beg you to do courageously and with fear of God what you have to do.'[46]

In 1378, Catherine became embroiled in yet another ecclesiastical crisis, this one precipitated by Pope Gregory XI's death. Those who pined after the Avignon-based papacy rejected the authority of the newly elected Urban VI, who was based in Rome. Instead, they set up a rival papacy, electing a Genevan, Clement VII, as an alternative Pope. The last eighteen months of Catherine's life were spent in Rome, 'devoting herself to the support of the lawful Pope,' and praying for an end to what became known as the 'Great Schism' – an impasse that ultimately outlived her.[47]

In fact, Muessig suggests that 'Catherine's constant activity as peacemaker, papal advisor, spiritual counsellor, and theologian' – in conjunction with 'her

---

46 Noffke, *Letters*, 1:250.

47 G. Cavallini, *Catherine of Siena* (London: Geoffrey Chapman, 1998), p. xxv.

brutal ascetic regime' – quickened her demise.[48] She died at noon on 29 April 1380 at the age of thirty-three, with her mother Lapa alongside her. One of her *famiglia,* Barduccio di Piero Canigani, was also present. He described the way, during the last days of her life, her frame 'was reduced to such a state that it seemed like a corpse in a picture, though I speak not of the face, which remained ever angelical and breathed forth devotion.' Her body itself was emaciated: 'nothing could be seen but the bones, covered by the thinnest skin, and so feeble was she from the waist downwards that she could not move herself, even a little, from one side to another.'[49] She died with Jesus' words on her lips: 'Father, into your hands I commit my soul and spirit.'[50]

My Book
It's been said that the past is a foreign country, and this is most certainly apparent when it comes to what we can learn from Catherine of Siena's short, though remarkably full, life. In her own day, far from being rebuked for unhelpful aspects of her theology and the harmful ascetic practices it prompted, she was promoted as nothing short of a cult hero and model of the faithful Christian life.

---

48 C. Muessig, 'Introduction' in C. Muessig, G. Ferzocco and B. Kienzle (eds.), *A Companion to Catherine of Siena* (Leiden: Brill, 2011), p. 9.

49 Catherine of Siena, *The Dialogue of Catherine of Siena,* trans. A. Thorold (London: Kegan Paul, Trench, Trubner & Co., 1907), p. 338.

50 Cavallini, *Catherine,* p. xxvi.

Even today, the Roman Catholic Church has done much to celebrate and remember her contributions: she was canonised in 1461 and in 1970 was named a 'Doctor of the Church' (someone recognised as having made a significant contribution to theology; she was one of only four women to have received this distinction).

In practice, Catherine thought self-denial was the avenue to the intimacy with Jesus that she – and we – long to experience. And yet, although her theology was undoubtedly a very mixed bag, those in the Protestant, evangelical tradition have much to learn from her colourful career. Acutely aware of the reality of the spiritual realm, her intense hatred of sin – especially her own – was exceeded only by the intense love she had for her Saviour-Spouse, who willingly took this burden upon Himself so that she – and we – might be forgiven.

Living in an era afflicted by wave after wave of the deadly *yersinia pestis bacillus* – the Black Death – Catherine's love for God and neighbour was both contagious and irrepressible. She has gifted the church with one of the most memorable and creative ways of describing the indissoluble, spiritual union we have with Jesus through faith: 'For then the soul is in God and God in the soul, just as the fish is in the sea and the sea in the fish, so am I in the soul and the soul in me, the sea of peace.'[51]

---

51 Noffke, *Dialogue,* p. 211.

She has also gifted God's people with a constructive and vibrant example 'for understanding how powerful and passionate and public criticism can be absolutely consistent with deep love and loyalty for the church.'[52] Catherine spoke biblical truth – often hard truth – in love and in the direction of high ecclesiastical places. 'So I hasten to you, our father and our shepherd,' she wrote to Pope Gregory in February 1376, 'begging you on behalf of Christ crucified to learn from Him.' She longed for church reform – that the bride of Christ would live up to its high calling – a renewal motivated by Jesus' sacrificial example, 'who with such fire of love gave Himself to the shameful death of the most holy Cross, to rescue that lost sheep, the human race.'[53]

'It is not possible… to remember the names of all the hard-hearted sinners [Catherine] brought back to belief,' reflected Raymond. Nor the identities of:

> All the lovers of the world she taught to despise it, all the people tempted by every kind of temptation whom her prayers and wisdom she saved from the wiles of the Devil; all those called by heaven whom she directed into the way of virtue; all those filled with holy intention whom she helped to look for still greater graces.'[54]

---

52 Anderson, *Catholic Reformers,* p. 122.

53 Noffke, *Letters,* 3:160-163.

54 Raymond, *Catherine,* p. 192.

From his vantage point as Catherine's mentor and confidant, Raymond of Capua was perhaps better positioned than anyone else to offer this summation of her life. She may have referred to *The Dialogue* as 'my book,' but ultimately her *magnum opus* was composed of the countless lives she was employed by God to bless.

For Further Reading

Raymond of Capua, *The Life of St. Catherine of Siena* (Charlotte, NC: Tan Books, 2003).

Giuliana Cavallini, *Catherine of Siena* (London: Geoffrey Chapman, 1998).

Chapter 4: Jane Grey
After Darkness, I Hope for Light

Rachel Ciano

From her window in the Tower of London, Lady Jane Grey, formerly the first Queen of England, watched as her husband, Guildford Dudley, was led out to his execution on Tower Hill.[1] He was up first; her turn was next. She refused his request to meet beforehand, because, as one contemporary explained, 'their meeting would only tend to increase their misery and pain...they would meet shortly elsewhere, and live bound by indissoluble ties.'[2] Guildford shared her evangelical faith; their part in this

---

1   There is ongoing debate about whether Lady Jane Grey can rightly be called 'Queen.' For example, Edward VI's *Devise for Succession* naming Jane Grey as his chosen successor was legally questionable and she was never officially coronated. Nevertheless, she was proclaimed Queen by the Privy Council and signed her name 'Jane the Queene.' For the purposes of this chapter, I will refer to her as Queen, whilst acknowledging it is a complex issue.

2   Giovanni Francesco Commendone, *The Accession, Coronation and Marriage of Mary Tudor* (ed. C. V. Malfatti, Barcelona, 1956), p.49. Cited in Eric Ives, *Lady Jane Grey: A Tudor Mystery* (Chichester, West Sussex: Wiley-Blackwell, 2009), p.274.

movement sweeping across Europe led to this fateful day. He did not take a Roman Catholic confessor with him for support; Jane presumably knew this meant he had stood by his Protestant convictions. Once the grisly deed was done, Jane saw his corpse carried back to the Tower on a cart and brought to the chapel to be unloaded. Upon seeing his lifeless body, she reportedly said: 'Oh Guildford, Guildford, the foretaste is not so bitter that you have tasted and that I shall soon taste as to make my flesh tremble, but that is nothing compared to the feast that you and I shall this day partake in heaven.'[3]

This certainty that both she and her husband would enter heaven that day was not based on any sense that they deserved God's favour; instead, she recognised her dependence on Jesus Christ alone to forgive her sin and grant her access to God. In short, she had come to wholeheartedly embrace the evangelical faith, recently rediscovered in the sixteenth-century Reformation.[4]

---

3 George Howard, *Lady Jane Grey, and her Times,* (ed. F. C. Laird, 1822), p. 378, quoting Michelangelo Florio, *Historia de la vita e de la morte de l'illustriss. Signora Giovanna Graia gia regina eletta e publicata in Inghilterra e de la cose accadute in quel Regno dopo la morte del Re Edoardo VI* (Middleburg, 1607), p.76. c.f. Ives, *Jane Grey*, p.339n30. Ives thinks Florio too florid in his recollection here, however, given that Florio was Jane's Italian tutor, any flourish may be understandable. Florio was formerly a Franciscan friar in Italy, and when he became a Protestant he was imprisoned by the Inquisition. He escaped and fled to London, becoming the first pastor of the Italian church at Austin Friars. See Ives, *Jane Grey*, pp.65, 275.

4 While the term 'evangelical' is often associated with movements in the eighteenth century, the sixteenth-century English reformers often referred to themselves as 'evangelicals' or 'gospellers.'

Post tenebras spero lucem

Jane Grey reportedly scratched the words, *post tenebras spero lucem,* into the wall of her room shortly before her death on Friday, 12 February 1554. The words are Latin for 'after darkness, I hope for light.' She was only seventeen when she wrote them. They bore enormous significance for her and filled her mind in her last days, shown in the painstaking effort it would have taken to etch them into a solid wall with a pin.

This phrase had several layers of significance for Jane and others who took it as a motto of their convictions. At their most basic level, the words came from the Bible: Jerome's fourth-century translation of the Bible into Latin, known as the Vulgate, used these words for Job 17:12.[5] One modern English version of this verse reads, 'in the face of darkness light is near' (NIV). Amid Job's intense and extended suffering, he explores the idea of hope, desiring night to turn into day and declaring that even in darkness, light and hope are close at hand. As Jane faced death, Job's hope that light follows darkness was her hope too.

Jane's adoption of this phrase was loaded with theological weight for those with ears to hear. These words, *post tenebras spero lucem,* had become a slogan during the sixteenth-century Protestant Reformation

---

5   Vulgate comes from 'vulgar,' as in the common, everyday language understood by the people: it was a translation meant to be understood by the people of Jerome's day. By the sixteenth century, only well-educated people knew Latin.

movement, of which Jane Grey was a keen student and a key part in England. The shortened, zippier version, *post tenebras lux*, meaning 'after darkness, light', became the motto for the reformers and those who followed in their footsteps; for example, many Protestant institutions adopted it as their motto. The phrase was first associated with John Calvin's Geneva; it was the ancient motto of the city when he first arrived in 1536, and the shorter version soon after appeared on Genevan coins.

This slogan spread from Geneva and became more broadly associated with the Protestant movement, encapsulating how evangelicals understood their reform movement's time and place in history. For Protestants of this era, and ever since, the darkness that preceded the sixteenth century was understood as gospel darkness, and the light that came was understood as gospel light. The Roman Catholic Church's belief that faith in Christ brings salvation required the essential contribution of good works, including participation in the sacraments. Many men and women closely examining the Scriptures in this period came to rediscover what the Bible and the early church said about salvation – that it was faith *alone*, in Christ *alone*, known through Scripture *alone*, that was essential to understanding the gospel of grace *alone*. 'Alone' (*sola* in Latin) can be understood as the centre of the Reformation hurricane, the real sticking point, for 'alone' insists that Christ *exclusively* provides for His people what is necessary for a person to be reconciled to God. 'Alone' was so crucial to Reformation thought, as it ruled out the contribution to salvation of anything else, such as the Church, a priest, partaking in the sacraments, and good works.

The original Brexit

This Protestant Reformation took off in Germany in 1517 with an Augustinian friar, Martin Luther, challenging the Roman Catholic Church on how God forgives a person. These ideas soon spread throughout Europe. However, around 150 years before this, John Wycliff, an Oxford-based priest and professor, had already challenged Roman Catholic teachings in the fourteenth century and is often called 'the morning star of the Reformation.' Wycliff and his followers, the Lollards, faced strong opposition, and the Catholic Church condemned him as a heretic.[6] Amongst Wycliff's 'crimes' was his belief that the Bible should be read and understood by everyone in their mother tongue, which led him to translate the Bible into English. With the help of the Lollards, he copied and distributed Bibles throughout England. Although Wycliff died of natural causes in 1384, he would not remain in his resting place. The Roman Catholic Church posthumously condemned him at the

---

6   The Lollards potentially got their name from the sound they made when they quietly prayed – a 'lo-lo-lo' sound. It was a pejorative term, but it soon came to identify the movement that followed Wycliff's teachings. Wycliff and the Lollards dissented from Roman Catholic doctrine in crucial areas, such as affirming the authority of Scripture alone, rejecting transubstantiation and confession to a priest, and belief in an 'invisible church' rather than the 'visible' Roman Catholic Church.

Council of Constance in 1415; his bones were dug up, burned, and sent drifting away on the River Swift in the English Midlands.

However, the Lollard movement persisted to such an extent that in the reign of Henry VIII (1509–1547), court documents revealed that Lollardy was the most common religious charge people faced in England. Jane Grey was born during Henry VIII's reign in 1537, and Henry's religious policies shaped the world of Jane's early childhood. Henry VIII was not enthusiastic about the prospect of Luther's and other reformers' ideas taking hold in England. Henry had his chief minister, Roman Catholic Cardinal Thomas Wolsey, publicly burn copies of Luther's works outside St Paul's Cathedral on 12 May 1521 to mark Luther's excommunication at the Diet of Worms.[7] Five months later, on 11 October, Pope Leo X gave Henry the illustrious title 'Defender of the Faith' for writing 'Declaration of the Seven Sacraments Against Martin Luther.' Even today, the monarchs of England continue to use the 'Defender of the Faith' title, and the initials 'F.D.' from the Latin, *Fidei Defensor*, sit alongside their portrait on the back of English coins.

---

7   Thomas Wolsey's other titles included Lord Chancellor, papal legate (the pope's representative in a foreign land), and Archbishop of York (the second highest position in the English church, behind the Archbishop of Canterbury). Wolsey held huge power and sway in England in the early part of Henry VIII's reign. However, his failure to obtain an annulment for Henry's first marriage to Catherine of Aragon ultimately led to his swift downfall.

However, Henry was an idiosyncratic Roman Catholic. Not long after he became the 'Defender of the Faith' he broke ties with the pope and the church in Rome to try and realise his desire for a legitimate male heir.[8] In Henry VIII's day, no woman had yet sat on the English throne (Empress Matilda in the twelfth century was never crowned). However, three of Henry's four successors in the Tudor dynasty were female (Queen Jane Grey, Queen Elizabeth I, and Queen Mary I). Given that England was still recovering from the civil war of his father's day (Henry VII) and that this new Tudor dynasty was still in its early, shaky days, it was important to Henry that a male heir succeed him.

His first wife, Catherine of Aragon, had only produced one living daughter: Mary, the future Queen Mary I, who would execute Jane Grey to secure her throne. For now, however, Henry was not content for Mary to be his immediate successor. He failed to receive an annulment for this marriage from the pope, despite the best efforts of English churchmen, such as Cardinal Wolsey. Henry, therefore, needed a massive restructuring of the church in England that placed him (and his successors) at the head of the church, not the pope. Henry's Parliament passed a series of laws that effectively cut the English church from Rome and made it its own entity, culminating in the *Act of Supremacy* in 1534, declaring the English

---

8   If you have already read *10 Dead Guys You Should Know*, the story may sound familiar to you as we considered the life of Thomas Cranmer.

monarch the 'Supreme Head of the Church of England.' This break from Rome was momentous, and has, in more recent times, earned the title, 'the original Brexit.'

Henry VIII's marriage to Catherine was annulled on 23 May 1533, and his marriage to Anne Boleyn was declared legal five days later (they had secretly married in January of that year). Unfortunately, Anne gave birth to a girl, not a boy, on 7 September that year – Elizabeth. She would become one of England's greatest monarchs as Elizabeth I; however, her birth did not produce Henry's contentment. Anne went on to reportedly miscarry a baby boy, perhaps brought on by the stress of hearing that Henry had nearly been fatally injured in a riding accident. Soon after, Anne fell out of favour with Henry. As a result of concocted charges, she foreshadowed Jane Grey and lost her head in the Tower of London on 19 May 1536. Henry was again free to marry, which he did the next day to one of Anne's ladies-in-waiting, Jane Seymour.

Eighteen months later, on 12 October 1537, Jane Seymour gave birth to Edward, providing Henry with his sought-after male heir. Around five months before Edward's birth, Jane Grey was born. Jane and Edward's lives ran parallel to one another, and in the end, the death of one led to the death of the other. Poor Jane Seymour died from complications twelve days after giving birth to Edward, leaving Henry bereft. Henry married another three times, but always considered Jane Seymour the love of his life, and even after her death,

Henry insisted that Jane should feature in the painted family portrait. Jane Seymour was the only wife Henry gave a Queen's burial, and they are buried next to each other in St George's Chapel in Windsor Castle. Henry and Jane's only son would become King of England nearly ten years later, on 28 January 1547, following his father's death.

King Edward VI would shape the Church of England along Protestant lines, and this religious direction drastically affected Jane Grey's life. Despite becoming King at the age of nine, Edward's religious convictions were avowedly Protestant, and his circle of advisors were committed reformers. Despite Henry VIII's more conservative, Roman Catholic leanings, he seems to have been aware that the future of England would be Protestant. This foresight is particularly demonstrated in his appointment of Thomas Cranmer to be Edward's tutor, which meant Cranmer would help shape Edward's convictions.

During Edward's six-year reign, Cranmer implemented significant reform as the Archbishop of Canterbury. He did this most notably by producing the *Book of Common Prayer* in English (1549, with a revised edition in 1552), a set of *42 Articles* (1552) that outlined the Protestant faith in England, and *12 Homilies* (sermons) to be used in churches for the clear exposition of evangelical convictions. Cranmer had also helped produce the English Bible Henry VIII had officially endorsed in 1539 (called 'The Great Bible'). However, for all Protestantism's gains in England at this time, it still had a tentative hold, relying on Edward's successor for its continuation. But who would that be?

The elect lady

Jane Grey was undoubtedly in a royally-connected family; she was the great-granddaughter of King Henry VII through her mother, Lady Frances Brandon, whose mother, Mary, was the youngest of King Henry VIII's two sisters. In terms of Jane Grey's generation, she shared a birth year with Edward Tudor, her second cousin. Jane and Edward had other similarities; they both received a thorough and rigorous education, which included an intense study of the Scriptures, encouraged by their prominent Protestant tutors. Both were very young when they were required to make big decisions regarding their Protestant convictions, and both would be renowned for their rigorous faith in their youth. Both were thrust upon the throne of England at a tender age (Edward was nine, Jane was fifteen), and both were dead in their teenage years.

There were also differences. Whilst Edward was born into a royal family, Jane was born into a (mere!) noble family. Both her parents were English nobility, meaning she had access to power, wealth, and significantly, education. Five per cent of women received an education in Tudor England, and around 10 per cent of boys did. Jane was perhaps one of the best-educated women in England of her day. She was given a humanist education: an approach to learning and education in vogue in Europe then. One of its emphases was learning languages to understand better the original sources, the Bible chief among these. Humanists often learned Greek and Hebrew to study the Scriptures and other writings in closer detail. Jane was exceptionally skilled in and dedicated to acquiring languages. She was fluent in Greek, Latin, and presumably French, proficient in Italian, and off to a good start with Hebrew.

Convictions are often forged through personal connections, and Lady Grey's family had some strong, somewhat covert Protestant contacts that formed a web across Europe. At the family home in Bradgate Park, Leicestershire, quite a few prominent evangelicals would visit, and Jane would participate in conversations with these visitors.[9] Jane's royal family connections (she was fourth in line to the throne in Henry VIII's will) meant she moved into Sudeley Castle with Katherine Parr, Henry VIII's sixth wife, when he died in 1547. Until Katherine's death the following year, Jane spent a formative eighteen months as part of this evangelical household. Katherine herself was an evangelical, committed to the importance of the Bible, and writing, promoting, and being involved with various evangelical writing projects.[10] Jane also spent time with other evangelicals who were part of

9 Hugh Latimer lived 2 ½ miles away in Thurcaston, and so it is quite possible that Latimer and the Grey household were connected, and that Latimer was amongst these visitors.

10 See Ives, *Jane Grey*, pp.67–70 for examples of Katherine Parr's writing projects.

the household or who visited, people who would later support Jane and even publish her writings.[11] She would have also attended evangelical-styled morning and evening prayers each day.

Upon Katherine's death, Jane returned to her family home, where the Grey family's firm ties to the recently executed Thomas Cromwell would also prove critical. Cromwell was one of the most influential men in England, succeeding Cardinal Wolsey as Lord Chancellor, until he was beheaded in 1540 after falling out of favour with Henry VIII. Cromwell was a committed Protestant and, among other things, worked hard to get an English Bible into the hands of the English people. However, he is probably best known for advocating and orchestrating the systematic review, and then closure, of the monasteries across England; the closure was met with various strong opinions then, and has been ever since!

Connections to Cromwell gave the Grey family access to Protestant reformers on the Continent, particularly with Zürich and its lead reformer, Heinrich Bullinger. Jane wrote to him; three of those letters still survive. Jane even asked for his tips on how best to learn Hebrew; whatever he suggested, she seemed determined to try![12] She is full

---

11 Miles Coverdale would visit Sudeley Castle and would later publish some of her writings. Nicholas Throckmorton was another visitor, and later a supporter. Ives, *Jane Grey,* p. 70.

12 See Jane Grey to Heinrich Bullinger, July 12 1551 and July 7 1552. Hastings Robinson (ed.), *Original Letters Relative to the English Reformation,* 2 vols. (Cambridge: Cambridge University Press, 1846), 1:7–8.

of praise for him as a reformer, writer, preacher, and for practising what he preached – he had a far-reaching reputation as a godly man.[13]

She knew the geographical gulf between them, writing, 'I am at a great distance from you, the couriers are few, and news reaches me slowly.'[14] She also knew their greater social gulf, particularly of age and gender. Though part of English nobility, she was still a teenage girl writing to one of her heroes at a time when this was not socially acceptable. She was aware that 'feminine boldness' and 'temerity which is for the most part adverse to our better judgement' meant it was, at the very least, unusual for a young woman starting out in her studies to write to someone like Bullinger.[15] However, her respect for Bullinger and her eagerness to learn from him outweighed her hesitancy in writing to him.[16] Jane wrote to him:

> Oh! Happy me, to be possessed of such a friend and so wise a counsellor! (for as Solomon says, 'in the multitude of counsellors there is safety;' [quoting in Hebrew Proverbs 11:14]) and to be connected by the ties of friendship and intimacy with so learned a man,

13 For example, see Jane Grey to Heinrich Bullinger, before June 1553: Robinson, *Original Letters,* 1:9.

14 Jane Grey to Heinrich Bullinger, before June 1553: Robinson, *Original Letters,* 1:9.

15 Jane Grey to Heinrich Bullinger, before June 1553: Robinson, *Original Letters,* 1:10.

16 Jane Grey to Heinrich Bullinger, before June 1553: Robinson, *Original Letters,* 1:10–11.

so pious a divine [i.e. a minister or theologian], and so intrepid a champion of true religion![17]

She wrote to him in an elaborate Latin style and quoted Greek and Hebrew. Despite her protestations of her 'mediocrity,' 'infancy in learning,' and being 'girlish and unlearned,' she was skilled enough to converse with Bullinger in this way![18] She expressed humility in writing to him: 'Whatever the divine goodness [i.e. God] may have bestowed upon me, I ascribe solely to himself, as the chief and sole author of any thing in me that bears any semblance of what is good.'[19] Jane likened herself to 'the elect lady' whom the Apostle John addressed in his second letter, feeling all the happiness that went along with that.[20] She told Bullinger that the 'motive' of her 'unreserved requests [which] may carry with them an appearance of boldness' was 'that I may draw forth from the storehouse of your piety such instruction as may tend both to direct my conduct, and confirm my faith in Christ my Saviour.'[21] In other words, she wrote because she wanted to know Jesus more and live a life honouring him.

---

17 Jane Grey to Heinrich Bullinger, July 12 1551: Robinson, *Original Letters*, 1:5.

18 Jane Grey to Heinrich Bullinger, before June 1553: Robinson, *Original Letters*, 1:10.

19 Jane Grey to Heinrich Bullinger, July 12 1551: Robinson, *Original Letters*, 1:7.

20 Jane Grey to Heinrich Bullinger, July 12 1551: Robinson, *Original Letters*, 1:5–6., c.f. 2 John 1.

21 Jane Grey to Heinrich Bullinger, July 12 1551: Robinson, *Original Letters*, 1:6.

A year later she told him, 'You exhort me to embrace a genuine and sincere faith in Christ my Saviour.'[22] Given Jane's priorities, there was no higher praise to give him!

The crown is not my right

For all Henry VIII's hopes that a male heir would lead to a stable Tudor dynasty, King Edward VI's death at age fifteen on 6 July 1553 soon plunged the English realm into disarray. Henry VIII's oldest daughter, Mary, was the most natural heir. However, she was a staunch Roman Catholic, out of personal convictions, but also because her legitimacy as an heir depended on it! If Henry had remained married to her mother and not left the Roman Catholic Church, Mary would probably have been on the throne by now. However, powerful men who were desperate to keep England Protestant hatched a plan to try and make sure Jane Grey, not Mary, would become Queen. Chief among those manoeuvring to place Jane on the throne was Jane's father-in-law, the Duke of Northumberland. He was Lord President of the Council that helped young King Edward rule England and, therefore, he held sway in the royal court.

As Edward neared death, Northumberland made two bold moves. First, it is possible he manoeuvred for his son, Guildford, to marry Jane in May 1553, potentially believing that once Edward eventually died and Jane became Queen, Guildford would be beside

---

22 Jane Grey to Heinrich Bullinger, July 7 1552: Robinson, *Original Letters*, 1:8.

her as King.[23] Second, Northumberland, with the help of others on the Privy Council (the inner circle of advisors), assisted Edward to change his will to make Jane his heir. A cursory glance at his hastily drawn-up 'Succession Devise' (complete with last-minute edits) reveals Edward's plans to shore up a Protestant monarchy as his illness worsened.[24]

Fatefully, Edward changed the succession from 'Lady Jane's male heirs' to 'Lady Jane *and* her male heirs' which was legally questionable, having never passed through Parliament.[25] When Jane was summoned and informed of Edward's death and the 'Succession Devise,' she had no idea she had been named as Edward VI's successor. She fell crying, protesting, 'The crown is not my right and pleases me not. The Lady Mary is the rightful heir.'[26] Those on the Privy Council were shocked

---

23 Some historians argue that the marriage between Jane and Guildford was simply a court wedding between two young people, others speculate that Northumberland had more of a hand in orchestrating it. The marriage took place before Edward VI's health started to rapidly deteriorate, so at the very least, the marriage was not a last ditch effort to quickly place Guildford in line as King.

24 You can find this 'Succession Devise' easily enough online; look and you will see the changes, which have a rushed quality to them.

25 Italics added. Throughout this chapter, where sixteenth-century sources are quoted, language and spelling have been updated for clarity. For comparison with Edward VI's *Devise for Succession,* see Henry VIII's *Succession Acts: The Act of Succession* (1534), *The Second Succession Act* (1536), *Third Succession Act* (1543). These are available to view online in the UK Parliamentary Archives.

26 *Ambassades de Messieurs de Noailles en Angleterre,* (ed. R. A. de Vertot and C. Villaret, Leyden, 1763), ii.211. Cited in Ives, *Jane Grey,* p.187.

and confused by Jane's reaction. However, Jane soon gave way to pressure from her supporters. She and her new Privy Council moved to the fortress of the Tower of London, where monarchs stayed before their coronation and where power and position lay – if you controlled the Tower, you held the realm.

The nine-day Queen

When Jane was proclaimed Queen throughout London, there was ominous silence. Usually, the announcement of a new monarch was met with celebrations and bonfires. However, the people were expecting Princess Mary to be Queen; Jane was a relative unknown. Mary fled London before Jane's supporters could arrest her and rallied assistance at a safer distance. Mary's supporters included Roman Catholics and Protestants – even many evangelicals realised that Mary was the more lawful successor. Northumberland and his troops pursued Mary and what he presumed were her smaller forces. He sent a naval fleet to cut off Mary's potential escape to the Continent, but they mutinied because they had not been paid, not out of particular support for Mary as Queen. The mutiny proved the decisive blow to Northumberland's scheme.[27] Jane lost her government's support, and previous allies now fled the Tower of

27 J. D. Alsop, 'A Regime at Sea, The Navy and the 1553 Succession Crisis.' *Albion, A Quarterly Journal Concerned with British Studies* 24, no. 4 (1992), 577–90. https://doi.org/10.2307/4050667.

London, abandoning her. Northumberland knew his hopes and plans for Jane as Queen were dashed, and he eventually proclaimed Mary as Queen in her place. This proclamation for Mary was met with celebration – a stark contrast to Jane's reception. All of this tumult and treachery had taken nine days, and the fanciful dream of Jane the Queen turned into a nightmare.

Queen Mary I arrived in London in early August 1553. Soon after, Jane, her husband, and several prominent evangelicals, including Thomas Cranmer, were arrested for treason. Three months later, on 13 November, they were marched through London with an axeman at the head of the procession, on their way to a very public trial. He walked with his axe pointed outwards as a sign of presumed innocence until proven guilty. Once there, Jane and Guildford were charged with treason because they proclaimed Jane Queen and took over the Tower of London when Mary was rightfully Queen. Once found inevitably guilty, she was condemned either to be 'burned alive on Tower Hill or beheaded as the Queen should please.'[28] On their march back, and on Jane's last walk outside the Tower walls, the axeman had his blade turned in – they were guilty.

Despite Jane's condemnation, Queen Mary may have been willing to be lenient towards her. Her execution was suspended, and she could have remained a prisoner

---

28   Ives, *Jane Grey*, p.252.

in the Tower of London indefinitely, which had various ways of accommodating prisoners, some reasonably comfortable. Jane occupied different parts of the Tower complex during the next three months and even spent some time living in the gaoler's house. She spent her time studying the Bible and had access to writing materials, her letters revealing her heart and continuing convictions. These prison letters were steeped in Scripture; one letter section shows a biblical allusion every nine words.[29] Out of all the passages she quoted, it is Matthew 10 she repeated most: Jesus' call to discipleship amidst the harsh realities of rejection and persecution, and the call to take up one's cross and follow Him. Jane wrote, 'What cross? The cross of infamy, and shame, of misery and poverty, of affliction and persecution for his name's sake.'[30]

Perhaps out of a desire to be remembered, she scratched various verses into the wall with a pin. As well as 'after darkness I hope for light,' she also etched:

Don't think it strange,
What can happen to a person.
If fate is this way for me,
The same may happen to you.

---

29 Ives, *Jane Grey,* p. 253.

30 Lady Jane Grey, *An Epistle of the Ladye Jane, a righte vertuous woman* (London: John Day, 1554), RSTC 7279, A.v^v–vi^r.

And:

> If God helps you,
> Malice shall not hurt you.
> If God does not help you,
> Then heavy labour shall not save you.[31]

Despite restrictions on exercise and company (she mostly wasn't allowed to talk to her husband!), Jane was at least kept alive in the Tower. However, as Queen Mary moved towards creating an alliance with Roman Catholic Spain by marrying Phillip II, evangelicals feared the religious and political direction England was heading. As a result, several uprisings called for Queen Mary's removal, but one such uprising, led by Thomas Wyatt, made it all the way to London. At this, Mary became convinced that while Jane was kept alive, her throne was in danger – Jane had to die.

I affirm that faith alone saves

Jane's impending execution on 12 February 1554 was now days away, and Queen Mary sent Roman Catholic theologian John Feckenham to dissuade her from her beliefs. This three-day meeting ranged through important theological questions. A transcript of the debate was smuggled out and later printed by Protestants who fled

---

31 Author's translation. Originally recorded in Latin, with English translation provided in John Foxe, *Actes and Monuments* (London: John Day, 1563), RSTC 11222, p.922. See also Ives, *Jane Grey,* p. 253.

England and Mary's harsh persecution of Protestants, which persecution earned her the nickname, 'Bloody Mary.' Key debate topics included Jane's belief in justification by faith alone, and a view of the Lord's Supper that rejected the Roman Catholic understanding of transubstantiation, all buttressed by her reliance on the Scriptures.[32] When Feckenham told her, 'it is necessary for salvation to do good works also, and it is not sufficient only to believe' Jane replied, 'I deny that, and I affirm that faith alone saves.'[33] When pressed about transubstantiation, she answered:

> God forbid that I should say that I eat the very natural body and blood of Christ, for then either I should pluck away my redemption, or else there were two bodies, or two Christs. One body was tormented on the cross, and then if they did eat another body, then he had two bodies. Or if his body was eaten, then it was not broken upon the cross…I pray you answer me this one question: Where was Christ when he said, 'Take, eat, this is my body?' Was he not at the table when he said so? He was at that time alive, and did not suffer until the next day…What did he take, but bread? What did he break, but bread? What did he give, but bread?[34]

---

32 Transubstantiation is the belief that although the accidents (the physical aspects) of the bread and wine remain (i.e. colour, texture, taste etc.), the substance of the bread and wine are converted ('transubstantiated') into the body and blood of Jesus.

33 *An Epistle of the Ladye Jane,* B.iii[r].

34 *An Epistle of the Ladye Jane,* B.iv[r]–B.iv[v].

Feckenham then challenged her on the apparent error of grounding her faith 'not upon the church, to whom you ought to give credit' to which she answered:

> No, I ground my faith on God's Word, and not upon the church. For if the church be a good church, the faith of the church must be tried by God's Word; and not God's Word by the church...Shall I believe the church because of antiquity? Or shall I give credit to that church, which takes away from me half of the Lord's Supper, and will not let any layperson receive it in both kinds?[35]

For Jane Grey to insist that God's Word was the bedrock of her faith, not the Roman Catholic Church, was monumental. The Roman Catholic Church of Jane's day, as well as today, affirms the authority of the Bible, but it must be interpreted by the hierarchical Church (technically, the 'Magisterium' – popes, and in turn, bishops), and the Bible is not the totality of God's Word, for Tradition is also a source of authority.[36] In her debate with Feckenham, Jane flips the argument. It is not the church that must assess the Bible, but rather the Bible must examine the church. She refused to give way to the argument that because the Roman Catholic Church found its historical, authoritative roots in antiquity via

---

35 *An Epistle of the Ladye Jane,* B.iv^v–B.v^r.

36 See, for example, *The Catechism of the Catholic Church* (1992), 85. 'The task of interpreting the Word of God authentically has been entrusted solely to the Magisterium of the Church, that is, to the Pope and to the bishops in communion with him.' *CCC,* 100.

apostolic succession, it must be believed. Rather, for Jane, it was apostolic authority as found in the Scriptures that held sway. This belief in the authority of Scripture alone, which Jane held fast to, was in contrast to the notion of the authority of the Roman Catholic Church coming from an unbroken chain of spiritual succession from the Apostle Peter. The trustworthiness of the Bible alone as true and authoritative for everything necessary for salvation brought her real comfort throughout her life, and as she faced her death.

Jane Grey stood in good company with other evangelicals of this period and ever since, in insisting that lay people receive both the bread and the wine at the Lord's Supper. Protestant Reformers strongly insisted upon communion in both kinds; by contrast, the Roman Catholic Church insisted the laity only receive the bread, for transubstantiation meant that in the body of Jesus (the bread) was the whole of Christ, making receiving His blood in the wine redundant. The comfort of partaking in the Lord's Supper, and receiving both bread and wine, is a wonderful legacy that the Reformers have bequeathed to us. It nourishes us spiritually as we recall the death of Jesus, meditate on the significance of His sacrifice for us and assures us of our salvation; just as real as the bread and wine that we taste and eat, so real is the fact that Jesus died on the cross for us.

The same day the debate ended, Stephen Gardiner, a staunch conservative and Protestant opponent, preached before Queen Mary. He condemned the uprising led by Thomas Wyatt and called for evangelicalism to be wiped out to ensure England's safety, which could not happen 'unless the rotten and hurtful members thereof were cut off and consumed.'[37] Jane's fate was now sealed. Tomorrow, she and her husband would have their heads cut off, and gallows were erected across London where over 100 rebels were hanged, some quartered afterwards. Wyatt's head was put on a spike over the entrance to the city, and a visitor to the city remarked, 'one sees nothing but gibbets [gallows] and hanged men.'[38]

That night, her last on this earth, Jane sent her sister her Greek New Testament. Inside, she had written:

I have here sent you, good sister Katherine, a book, which although it is not outwardly trimmed with gold, yet inwardly it is of more worth than precious stones. It is the book, dear sister, of the law of the Lord...if you with a good mind read it, and with an earnest desire follow it, it shall bring you to an immortal and everlasting life. It will teach you to live and learn you to die...If you diligently apply this book, seeking to direct your life after it, you shall be an inheritor of such riches...that neither the thief shall steal, nor the moths corrupt.[39]

---

37 John Gough Nichols, *The Chronicle of Queen Jane and of Two Years of Queen Mary* (London: J.B. Nichols and Son, 1850), p.54.

38 The Spanish ambassador, Simon Renard wrote this remark on 17 February, five days after Jane Grey's execution. Cited in Peter Marshall, *Heretics and Believers* (New Haven: Yale University Press, 2017), p.372.

39 *An Epistle of the Ladye Jane*, B.vi^r–Bvi^v.

Leaving this mortal life

She woke up on 12 February 1554, knowing this was the day of her execution. Six months earlier at her gaoler's dinner table in the Tower, Jane said: 'Should I, who am young and few in my years, forsake my faith for the love of life? No, God forbid!…But God be merciful to us, for he says, "Whoever denies him before men, he will not know him in his Father's kingdom."'[40]

Now, her conviction would be put to the test. After seeing Guildford's headless body pass by, she walked to the newly erected scaffold within the Tower, clutching her miniature prayer book and praying along the way.[41] Inside, she wrote a message to the lieutenant of the Tower to whom she was bequeathing it, encouraging him to remember that he too would die, and to be spiritually prepared.[42] Jane and Guildford both wrote messages to her father, Henry Grey, inside it too.[43] Jane wrote in tiny, impeccable handwriting, 'Trust that we by leaving this mortal life have won an immortal life,' and Guildford

---

40 Nichols, *Chronicle,* pp. 25–6. A guest at the gaoler's dinner table that day recorded Jane's words. The author was perhaps a fellow prisoner in the Tower, or in royal service whose work took them to the Tower, or perhaps even a bishop. Whoever they were, they give an important firsthand account of the last days of Jane's life.

41 A copy of this tiny prayer book, measuring 85x70mm, can be viewed digitally via the British Library website: http://www.bl.uk/manuscripts/FullDisplay.aspx?ref=Harley_MS_2342. The scaffold was most likely erected on the northwest corner of the central White Tower, a short distance and in full view from where Jane was held.

42 See British Library, MS Harley 2342, fols. 74^v–77^r.

43 Jane and Guildford's inscriptions can be seen respectively in British Library, MS Harley 2342, fols. 78^r–80^r; 59^v–60^r.

scrawled, 'Your loving and obedient son wishes unto your grace long life in this world…and in the world to come joy everlasting.'[44] Henry Grey was executed less than two weeks later.

Jane remained calm, even as her ladies-in-waiting wept. She climbed the scaffold and addressed the small crowd: 'I pray you will all bear me witness, that here I die a true Christian woman, and that I trust to be saved by the blood of Jesus Christ, and by no other means.'[45] She conceded the justice of her sentence, as was expected of the condemned. She admitted she was wrong to take the crown but declared she had never desired it. She knelt and prayed Psalm 51 from her prayer book, asking God to have mercy. She then stood, thanked those around her for their kindness, and passed on her prayer book, which was an expected token of thanks from the doomed. Jane forgave the executioner for what he was about to do and placed her head on the executioner's block, apparently guided by Feckenham when she struggled to find it.[46] Blindfolded, she stretched out her body, head in position, and uttered her final words, 'Lord, into your hands I commend my spirit.'[47]

---

44 British Library, MS Harley 2342, fols. 79ʳ; 59ᵛ–60ʳ.

45 *An Epistle of the Ladye Jane,* B.viiiʳ.

46 Feckenham was there at the execution in case Jane wanted to convert to Roman Catholicism, and because no Protestant chaplain was allowed. He served as a witness and representative for Queen Mary.

47 Nichols, *Chronicle,* p.59.

Throughout this account of Lady Jane Grey's life, we have seen various ways she models robust faith for us. First, her heartfelt diligence and commitment to studying the Scriptures were fuelled by a desire to live a life worthy of her calling as a Christian. This is seen, for example in her letters to Bullinger. Second, her tenacity and steadfastness in debating Feckenham demonstrate her firm grasp of fundamental truths evangelicals hold dear, such as a reliance on the Scriptures and a firm belief that faith alone saves. Third, her calm, gracious conduct in death shows a woman ready to meet her end, a calmness that comes from knowing that heaven awaits her because of God's mercy, not her own goodness. Her words, 'after darkness, I hope for light,' were realised in her own life and death and in the light of gospel truths that continued to go forth after her short life ended.

For further reading

Faith Cook, *Nine Day Queen of England: Lady Jane Grey* (Darlington, Co Durham: Evangelical Press, 2004).

Eric Ives, *Lady Jane Grey: A Tudor Mystery* (Chichester, West Sussex: Wiley-Blackwell, 2009).

Chapter 5: Anne Hutchinson
A Woman Unfit for Our Society

Ian Maddock

The Siwanoy tribe had given plenty of advance warning that they were coming to raze the small settlement in New Netherland (in what is today the Bronx, New York). Their chief, Wampage, didn't expect to find any lingering inhabitants, but when they arrived that August day in 1643, they discovered one house still occupied. Without hesitation, they scalped everyone inside, most of them members of one family, the oldest of whom was a single, middle-aged mother: Anne Hutchinson. At the time of her grisly death, Hutchinson was arguably the most infamous British woman in the American colonies, having been found guilty of heresy and banished from the Massachusetts Bay Colony five years earlier. Her reputation preceded her. It was customary for Native American chiefs to adopt the name of their most high-profile victim, and in a testimony to Hutchinson's notoriety, Wampage became known thereafter as 'Anne Hoeck.'

When news of her violent demise filtered back to the governing authorities in Boston, they could scarcely hide their sense of self-righteous vindication: she got what she deserved. One minister rejoiced in God's providential justice: 'I never heard that the Indians in those parts did ever before this commit the like outrage upon any one family or families, and therefore God's hand is the more apparently seen herein, to pick out this woeful woman... Thus the Lord heard our groans to heaven, and freed us from our great and sore affliction.' Another saw a salutary warning in her fate: 'Let her damned heresies, and the just vengeance of God, by which she perished, terrify all her seduced followers from having any more to do with her leaven.'[1]

But if Anne Hutchinson was reviled in death, in recent times her legacy has undergone a remarkable transformation. Today she is revered as a virtual American founding mother, willing to challenge the seventeenth-century Puritan male-dominated state-church nexus at immense personal cost. In a twist that surely nobody could have foreseen during Hutchinson's lifetime, before one can view the portrait of her chief accuser, Governor John Winthrop, located within the present-day Massachusetts State House, one must first pass by a statue erected in Hutchinson's honour! Once excommunicated

---

1   E. LaPlante, *American Jezebel* (New York: HarperCollins, 2004), pp. 243-244.

and cast out as an 'American Jezebel,'[2] a woman 'unfit for our society,'[3] she is now memorialised in bronze as a 'courageous exponent of civil liberty and religious toleration.'[4] In a final act of retrospective rehabilitation, in 1987, then Governor of Massachusetts, Michael Dukakis, pardoned Hutchinson, formally overturning the judgment made by his predecessor Winthrop 350 years earlier.

How did this complex British woman – variously abhorred and adored – find herself enmeshed in a controversy that threatened to tear apart the social fabric that held together the Puritan experiment's "city upon a hill" in Boston? And what further events transpired for her to settle at an even newer frontier British settlement in Rhode Island, only to uproot once more and soon afterwards perish as the collateral damage of a Dutch-Native American conflict?

Like mother, like father, like daughter

Anne Hutchinson was born in Alford, Lincolnshire, in July 1591. She was the third of twelve children born to Francis Marbury – a Church of England minister with Puritan sensibilities and an appetite for ecclesiastical conflict – and Bridget Dryden, a midwife. As we shall soon see, many of the dramatic turns in Anne's life were

---

2 LaPlante, *American Jezebel*, p. 245.

3 T.D. Hall, *Anne Hutchinson: Puritan Prophet* (Boston: Longman, 2010), p. 122.

4 The statue, dedicated in 1922, bears this inscription.

foreshadowed in her parents' vocations and experiences: like mother, like father, like daughter. The importance of education in the Marbury household can't be overstated. Her father doubled as a schoolteacher as well as a minister, and made a point of teaching not just his sons but his daughters too. As a young, recently ordained minister in Northampton, Francis also made a point of publicly condemning the spiritually lethal results of the lack of education among Church of England clergy: 'I say the bishops of London and Peterborough and all the bishops of England are guilty of the death of as many souls as have perished by the ignorance of the ministers of their making whom they knew to be unable.'[5] In the heresy trial that unsurprisingly soon followed in 1578, his ecclesiastical superiors described him variously and colourfully as an 'ass,' 'mad,' 'courageous', and a 'knave,' before throwing him in gaol. 'Did you ever hear one more impudent?' asked one bishop – words that could easily have been uttered by Anne's accusers at her own heresy trial in Boston, nearly sixty years later.[6]

Marbury was anything but idle during his two-year incarceration. Instead, he took the opportunity to compose a gripping account of his high-risk, low-reward standoff, where he cast himself as a witty and savvy deployer of Scripture who bettered his opponents, but was nonetheless silenced. Anne read and internalised this Marbury family folklore, and in the process inherited

5   LaPlante, *American Jezebel*, p. 23.
6   Ibid., p. 24.

not just her father's scriptural literacy but also his proclivity for defiance under duress.

Another trial and imprisonment would follow – this time a three-year house arrest at his new parish in Alford. But in 1605, with his numerous clerical run-ins seemingly forgiven and forgotten, the Marbury family moved down to London where Francis had been appointed vicar of St Martin in the Vintry. Anne spent her teenage years on the north side of the Thames, just across the river from the Globe Theatre. It's almost certain she never attended one of Shakespeare's plays – the theatre and its risqué content would have been off-limits for a minister's daughter – but she probably recognised him: the playwright lived nearby, and his journey to and from the famous playhouse would have taken him past the vicarage each day.

From England to New England
A year after her father's death, in 1612 Anne 'moved from one high achieving godly family to another' when she married a wealthy textile merchant and fellow Alford local, William Hutchinson.[7] They didn't remain in London long, leaving behind their urban existence and settling back in their hometown. Their relocation coincided with the arrival of the celebrated up-and-coming preacher, John Cotton, in nearby Boston (the original Lincolnshire version!). In an era when commuting to church was

7   M.P. Winship, *Making Heretics: Militant Protestantism and Free Grace in Massachusetts, 1636-1641* (Princeton: Princeton University Press, 2002), p. 38.

virtually non-existent, the Hutchinsons regularly travelled the roughly twenty miles (a twelve-hour round trip) to hear Cotton preach.

For the next two decades, Anne amplified Cotton's emphasis on the unconditional and unmerited free grace of God in private gatherings in her home (known as conventicles). In an era when women had no formal public voice, these meetings were one of the few venues where talented women like Anne were able to exercise their teaching gifts. If Anne greatly admired Cotton, then the feeling was mutual. Just as Anne helped reinforce Cotton's teaching, then in turn, Cotton reinforced Anne's deft fusion of midwife and evangelist/theologian. 'She did much good in child-birth travails,' he wrote, 'and readily fell into good discourse with the women about their spiritual estates.'[8] Cotton rejoiced in the influence her ministry had upon men too, reflecting on how 'she had more to resort to her for counsel about matters of conscience and clearing up men's spiritual estates, than any minister' he knew.[9] Anne's attempt to replicate this ministry – and doctrine – in New England would be the catalyst for the events that followed, and the reason we still know of her today.

John Cotton was always a reluctant member of the Church of England at heart. His ability to fly under the ecclesiastical radar came to an end in 1632, when the new Archbishop of Canterbury, William Laud, signalled

8   La Plante, *American Jezebel,* p. 87.
9   Ibid., p. 87.

his intention to flush out and expel all ministers who refused to comply with his theological and liturgical flavour of Anglicanism. Faced with losing his ministry and even excommunication, in 1633 Cotton left one Boston for another, joining in the flood of like-minded Puritans and non-conformists who emigrated to New England during what became known as the Great Migration. He would soon become one of the main architects of Congregationalism as the preferred form of church governance in Massachusetts, renouncing Anglicanism's episcopal structure.

But the Cotton-Hutchinson partnership wouldn't be separated for long. A year later, in 1634, Anne, William, and their eleven children (a twelfth surviving child would later be born in America) followed their beloved minister across the Atlantic. Hutchinson picked up in New England right where she'd left off in England. As prosperous, high-status members of society, Mister and Mistress Hutchinson (people of lower rank were typically addressed as Goodman and Goodwife) were in the public eye from the moment they arrived. William's business acumen allowed them to settle alongside the most prominent Boston families on Shawmut Peninsula (today's downtown Boston) and, soon after their arrival, he was elected to serve on the General Court. John Winthrop, who would serve many terms as Governor – and in due course preside over Anne's trial and banishment – lived directly across the road.

Anne immediately gained a reputation not just for her skills as a midwife, but also for her ability to critically interrogate that week's sermon before rapidly growing – and, controversially, mixed gender – audiences in her home. She was not afraid to take sides in a rapidly escalating theological conflict between proponents of a 'covenant of works' and a 'covenant of grace.' The former was represented by John Winthrop and many of the colony's religious leaders, including one of the ministers at the First Church in Boston, John Wilson. Hutchinson supported the latter position, which was represented by, among others, her brother-in-law John Wheelwright, and Henry Vane (who would go on to defeat Winthrop in the 1636 Governor's race). In seventeenth-century Massachusetts, all theology was political, and all politics were theological!

The Antinomian Controversy

The ensuing fracas became known as the Antinomian (or Free Grace) Controversy, and between 1636 and 1638 it threatened the social cohesion of this fragile new society. Ever since the Reformation, Protestants had taught that although salvation is by God's free grace through faith alone, at the same time true faith is never alone; rather, true faith is always accompanied by works that visibly demonstrate the authenticity of one's verbal profession of faith. But instead of being viewed as mutually reinforcing truths that accentuate the inseparability of justification and sanctification, in

Boston they were pitted against one another and came to be seen as mutually exclusive positions – shibboleths of either orthodoxy or heresy depending upon which stance you supported. And while both camps spent much time contending for their respective positions, they also devoted considerable energy contending against the threats – both real and perceived – posed by the other.

For those aligned with the idea that true faith is never alone – 'sanctificationists' as Hall describes them – the threat of antinomianism (literally, 'against' or 'opposed to the law') loomed large.[10] Their fear was that 'free gracers' – Hutchinson, Vane, and company – 'were trying to hijack their godly commonwealth, turning it into a place of anarchy and licentiousness.'[11] Maintaining social cohesion was paramount, and emphasising the 'covenant of works' was a practical way of achieving that. Conversely, those who advocated for the 'covenant of grace' feared that Winthrop, Wilson, and company had functionally made a person's standing before God dependent upon good works, undoing the very essence of the Reformers' reclamation of salvation by grace *alone*. Some, like Anne's long-time mentor John Cotton (also a minister at the First Church in Boston alongside Wilson), occupied a precarious middle ground and repeatedly attempted to broker peace, but to little avail.

---

10 Hall, *Anne Hutchinson*, p. 86.
11 Ibid., p. 86.

At their core, both parties were preoccupied with finding a satisfactory answer to the same question: how can we be assured of being in God's favour? If the 'sanctificationists' tended to look outwards for external evidence, then the "free gracers" tended to look inwards for internal evidence. During Vane's short-lived governorship between 1636 and 1637, those who emphasised that the 'inward witness of the Holy Spirit' was sufficient proof of one's election had a privileged place at the table in Massachusetts society. But when Winthrop regained his position as Governor, he swiftly had her relative and fellow 'free gracer,' John Wheelwright, banished for sedition, an omen of what lay in store for Hutchinson.

Winthrop goes heresy hunting
The Massachusetts General Court handed down its verdict on Hutchinson's brother-in-law on 3 November 1637. Just four days later, her own civil trial would begin. She had lived under the shadow of suspicion for some time. The gatherings of up to eighty men and women she presided over in her home (Henry Vane was a notable and regular attendee) had long been suspected by her detractors to be hotbeds of dissension and even marital infidelity. Hutchinson's presumed guilt by Wheelwright-association didn't help her cause either. Winthrop was in no doubt: for all of the many disputing actors at play in this colonial drama, Anne Hutchinson was the

ringleader, 'the head of all this faction... the breeder and nourisher of all these distempers.'[12]

As both judge and prosecutor of the trial, Winthrop was determined to see Hutchinson 'reduced' – that is, repent – or else be banished. He opened proceedings by laying out the Court's case against her, a case immediately conspicuous for its lack of first-hand evidence and its reliance on hearsay: 'You are called here as one of those that have troubled the peace of the commonwealth and the churches here,' began Winthrop. He continued, 'You have been known to be a woman that has a great share in the promoting and divulging of those opinions that are causes of this trouble, and ... you have spoken diverse things as we have been informed is very prejudicial to the churches and ministers thereof.'[13]

As a woman, Anne was not entitled to legal representation and was forced to defend herself before a phalanx of magistrates, clergy, and deputies: upwards of sixty black-clad men arrayed against a lone mother of twelve. But if Hutchinson was outnumbered, this daughter of Francis Marbury was anything but outmatched. Undaunted by the prospect of days of unrelenting legal and biblical sparring, Anne immediately put her accusers on the back foot. She recognised that the case against her rested largely on second-hand evidence and

---

12   E. Battis, *Saints and Sectaries: Anne Hutchinson and the Antinomian Controversy in the Massachusetts Bay Colony* (Chapel Hill, NC: University of North Carolina Press, 1962), pp. 188-89.

13   LaPlante, *American Jezebel,* p. 12.

insinuation: 'I have been called here to answer you, but hear no things laid to my charge... what have I said or done?'[14] Knowing full well that since all of her utterances were made in private – and no formal written record of them existed – as long as she didn't incriminate herself, proving the charges against her would be very difficult. She might still be found guilty of course, but such an outcome would be a perversion of justice, the triumph of ecclesial and political might over right.

As the trial unfolded over two full days, Hutchinson – six months pregnant and standing throughout – repeatedly thwarted her accusers. The conventicles that Anne hosted at the Hutchinson family home came under particular scrutiny, especially with regard to the way she reputedly used these occasions to criticise the doctrinal content of John Wilson's sermons, and even cast doubt on whether other ministers like Hugh Peter had even been elected to receive salvation.

But it wasn't simply her theology that was under siege at the Newtown Meeting House; the fact that as *a woman* her theology had entered the public domain in the first place was an affront: she had behaved in a manner not 'comely in the sight of God nor fitting for [her] sex.'[15] Hall observes that 'English society took for granted that women were the weaker sex, more emotional and less capable of reason than men, although perhaps more religious, and it laid out narrow

14 Ibid., p. 13.
15 Ibid., p. 12.

roles for them' – assigned roles that Hutchinson had habitually flouted.[16] When challenged as to what right she had to adopt the role of a teacher, Anne responded, 'If any come to my house to be instructed in the ways of God, what rule have I to put them away?' 'Appealing to Paul's injunction in Titus 1, she asked 'Do you think it not lawful for to teach women?' Hutchinson even added an inflammatory rejoinder: besides, 'why do you call me to teach the court?' [17]

This last provocation was too much for Winthrop, who lost his composure and instinctively blurted, 'We do *not* call you to teach the court but to lay open yourself.' It was left to the colony's secretary, Simon Bradstreet – husband of the celebrated Puritan poet, Anne Bradstreet – to attempt to find some grounds for reconciliation. Conceding that there was, strictly speaking, nothing unlawful about these conventicles – nonetheless given the controversy they were inciting – as an act of goodwill, would she at least consider ceasing and desisting from this point onwards? Anne saw the prospect of compromise – and promptly rejected it! 'Sir, in regard of *myself* I could. But for *others* I do not yet see light, [although I] shall further consider it.'[18]

---

16 Winship, *Making Heretics*, p. 42.

17 LaPlante, *American Jezebel*, p. 48.

18 Ibid., p. 49.

By an immediate revelation

But despite Anne's feisty defence, the cards were always stacked against her. In many ways, the result of the trial was a foregone conclusion – in retrospect, these proceedings amounted to a guilty verdict in search of a court case. 'The outcome was not a surprise,' suggests Lindley. 'The only question about the process was how they would find grounds to convict Anne Hutchinson.'[19] What did come as a surprise was the way in which she succumbed, falling prey not to the questions of her accusers, but to her own unsolicited testimony about her sources of theological authority. It was an 'own goal' or 'unforced error' – not her opponent's superior offense – that eventually brought about her downfall.

If the leaders were alarmed at the extensive informal authority Hutchinson exercised in the community, they were equally concerned about *where* she located her ultimate source of theological authority. Her views on this matter had actually been the subject of suspicion as far back as 1634 while still in transit to Boston. Her claim to have received a vision confirming the exact date of the ship's arrival raised enough theological eyebrows that her admission to membership of the First Church in Boston was delayed while Cotton vouched for her credentials.

---

19 S.H. Lindley, *'You Have Stept Out of Your Place': A History of Women and Religion in America* (Louisville: Westminster John Knox Press, 1996), p. 4.

Now, once more, her orthodoxy was in question. Was her ultimate authority Scripture, mediated especially through male authority figures like the clergy and magistrates? Or did she functionally privilege her own private visions and inspirations over the written Word of God? The statue commemorating her outside the Massachusetts State House captures her ambivalence when it came to this question – on the one hand, clutching a Bible in her left hand, but her head lifted high, eyes gazing upwards at heaven as if expecting to receive direct revelation.

As the legal stalemate drifted on – and in a twist that appeared to stun the Court – Hutchinson suddenly gifted them with the proof they needed to convict her. Unprompted, Hutchinson began to proactively describe her theology of revelation, and in the process she fatefully volunteered that she considered herself able to discern truth 'by an immediate revelation' and 'by the voice of [God's] *own spirit* to my soul.'[20] Her critics smelt blood in the water: if anybody could do whatever 'their divine voices told them to,' then 'the end of all moral restraint, as well as the need for ministers or authorities of any kind' would inevitably follow.[21] Cotton attempted to rescue her: surely she simply meant that the illumination of the Holy Spirit is needed to properly interpret God's Word? But far from backing down – or even qualifying her previous

---

20 LaPlante, *American Jezebel*, p. 118.

21 M.P. Winship, *The Times and Trials of Anne Hutchinson* (Lawrence: University Press of Kansas, 2005), p. 112.

statements – Hutchinson doubled down and accused her accusers, citing an 'immediate revelation' she had received, one that 'doth concern you all.' Likening herself to Daniel – unjustly accused and delivered from the lion's den – she declared, 'the Lord bid me not to fear… And see! This Scripture [is] fulfilled this day in mine eyes!'[22]

Completely unshackled and firmly on the offensive, Anne threw caution to the wind (perhaps she sensed she was by now as good as banished) and laid down one final charge of her own. 'You have no power over my body, neither can you do me any harm—for I am in the hands of the eternal Jehovah, my Saviour,' she declared, before pronouncing a belligerent judgment of her own on those who would judge her:

> I fear none but the great Jehovah, which hath foretold me of these things, and I do verily believe that he will deliver me out of your hands. Therefore take heed how you proceed against me—for I know that, for this you go about to do to me, God will ruin you and your posterity and this whole state.[23]

Winthrop had promised Hutchinson at the outset that if she remained 'obstinate in [her] course,' then the 'court may take such course that you may trouble us no further.'[24] They came good on this vow with gusto. In the end, only a few deputies swam against the tide

---

22 LaPlante, *American Jezebel,* p. 120.

23 Ibid., pp. 120-121.

24 Ibid., p. 13.

and voted against banishing her. One of these, William Coddington, bravely went out on a limb and went so far as to call into question the legal legitimacy of the trial: 'I do not see any clear witness against her, and you know it is a rule of the court that no man may be a judge and an accuser too.'[25] For her part, Hutchinson's last words saw her circle back to her original line of defence: 'I desire to know wherefore I am banished?' Winthrop was curt and dismissive: 'Say no more, the court knows wherefore and is satisfied.'[26]

I command you as a Leper to withdraw

But Hutchinson's ordeal was not yet over. She might have been formally banished, but before she could leave there was still an ecclesiastical trial to come, where the clergy would decide whether or not to also excommunicate her from the Boston church. She spent the intervening four months under house arrest, separated from her family. By this stage, her husband and some other supporters had formed an advance party and set off towards Rhode Island, where Roger Williams – himself banished in 1636 – had established a settlement named Providence Plantations. Soon afterwards, in April 1638, she would walk sixty miles in deep snow to join them.

Hutchinson's second trial took place on 22 March 1638. With her banishment assured – and probably

---

25 R.B. Morris, 'Jezebel Before the Judges,' in F. Bremer (ed.), *Anne Hutchinson: Troubler of the Puritan Zion* (Huntington, NY: Robert E. Krieger, 1981), p. 63.

26 Hall, *Anne Hutchinson*, p. 122.

sensing the need to put daylight between himself and Hutchinson in order to buttress his own bona fides in the community – in a cruel turn of events, her mentor John Cotton made the final case for her excommunication. She was eventually found guilty of denying the bodily resurrection and thereby obliterating gender distinctions in the here and now, though whether she actually believed this is highly debatable. But it seems sifting the merits of Anne's convictions was never the real goal of the exercise – only securing her conviction of heresy.

First, her twenty-something son Edward and son-in-law Thomas were rebuked by Cotton for coming to their mother's defence: 'instead of loving and natural children you have proved vipers to eat through the very bowels of your mother – to her ruin,'[27] scolded Cotton. He then turned to Anne, admitting that since her arrival in Boston she had been 'an instrument of doing some good' – his emphasis being on *some* – before turning to the implied 'but' that surely followed. Indeed, this small measure of praise was more than offset by a ferocious barrage rendered all the more stunning given their decades of shared history and a friendship that spanned oceans. He declared her guilty of promoting 'that *filthy* sin of the community of women – and all promiscuous and *filthy* coming-together of men and women without distinction or relation of marriage,' before interpreting her 'desperate falls' as manifestations of God's justice: 'the Lord looketh

---

27 LaPlante, *American Jezebel,* p. 185.

upon all the children of pride and delights to abase them and bring them low.'[28]

Cotton's abandonment of Hutchinson carried a lot of weight, and – a few family members notwithstanding – the overwhelming majority of the church voted to add excommunication to her banishment. Perhaps with Hutchinson's blunt assessment of his dire spiritual state still fresh in his mind, Hugh Peter offered an equally blunt assessment of his own: Hutchinson 'had rather be a husband than a wife; a preacher than a hearer; and a magistrate than a subject.'[29] It was symbolically appropriate that John Wilson, whose doctrine Hutchinson had challenged, should be left with the duty of delivering the sentence: 'Forasmuch as you, Mrs. Hutchinson, have highly transgressed and offended... and troubled the Church with your Errors and have drawn away many a poor soul, and have upheld your Revelations,' he began:

> 'Therefore, in the name of our Lord Jesus Christ... I do cast you out and... deliver you up to Satan... and account you from this time forth to be a Heathen and a Publican.... I command you in the name of Christ Jesus and of this Church as a Leper to withdraw yourself out of the Congregation.[30]

With the eyes of the congregation upon her, Hutchinson began to walk – for the last time – down the centre

---

28 Ibid., pp. 188-189.
29 Hall, *Anne Hutchinson,* p. 135.
30 LaPlante, *American Jezebel,* pp. 204-205.

aisle of the meeting house towards the exit. In an act of solidarity, a lone woman, Mary Dyer, rose, joined her, and held her hand. It would soon be discovered that six months earlier, Hutchinson had been the midwife holding Dyer's hand as she gave birth to a stillborn girl with extensive deformities of the head, spinal column and limbs – anencephaly in modern medical terms, but a 'monstrous birth' in the language of their day – and interpreted as a sure sign of God's judgment on both the mother and midwife. With Dyer at her side, Hutchinson turned to her judges and uttered her first words as an outcast: 'The Lord judges not as man judges. Better to be cast out of the church than to deny Christ.'[31]

Misshapen opinions must bring forth deformed monsters

For the next five years, Hutchinson and a group of sympathisers established a community in Portsmouth, Rhode Island. Like Williams' nearby Providence Plantations, it offered a refuge for those seeking 'liberty of conscience' and a place where church and state were separated. But if she was now out of sight, she definitely wasn't out of mind of the authorities back in Boston. In fact, they made a point of carefully monitoring her movements through a program of remote surveillance.

When news filtered back to Boston that her most recent pregnancy had ended in a miscarriage – a 'monstrous birth' of her own – they were quick to seize on this as

---

31 Ibid., p. 207.

further vindication of their decision to banish her. Today the delivery would be classified as a 'hydatidiform mole,' not uncommon in middle-aged pregnancies, where 'sperm duplicates its own DNA after fertilizing an unformed ... mass of tissue.'[32] Just as Hutchinson had purportedly uttered her multiple heresies in public, Winthrop felt justified in reporting her 'monstrous birth' to the whole church the Sunday after he learned of it: 'But see how the wisdom of God fitted this judgement to her sin every way, for look – as she had vented misshapen opinions, so she must bring forth deformed monsters.'[33] Humiliated in absentia, it's little wonder that when three men arrived on her doorstep, announcing themselves to be representatives of the Boston church, she had little time for their offer to restore her should she repent. Hutchinson is said to have replied 'I know no such church... You may call it the 'Whore and Strumpet of Boston,' but no Church of Christ!'[34]

In 1641, Anne's husband of twenty-one years died. It coincided with an effort to bring Rhode Island back under the jurisdiction of the Massachusetts Bay Colony. This manoeuvre never eventuated, but 'Hutchinson and her family feared jail or worse should Massachusetts take over their colony.'[35] In 1642, with her seven youngest children, son-in-law, and several servants, she

---

32 Hall, *Anne Hutchinson,* p. 140.

33 LaPlante, *American Jezebel,* p. 218.

34 Ibid., p. 221.

35 Winship, *Times and Trials,* p. 145.

relocated from New England to the Dutch colony of New Netherlands.

Within a year all were dead, victims of a Native American reprisal against the settlement prompted by recent Dutch atrocities – all, that is, except nine-year-old Susanna. From all accounts she was picking blueberries at the time of the attack, and was discovered – and adopted – by the tribe. Susanna was eventually released, and she reintegrated into British society, going on to marry and settle in Boston, as the stigma associated with the Hutchinson name began to recede in the community's collective memory.

More Bold than a Man

In a time and place where, aside from records of their births, deaths, and marriages, women left virtually no imprint on the written landscape, Anne Hutchinson refused to be invisible. Her story – simultaneously exhilarating and tragic, daring and doomed – allows us to view the religious and social world of seventeenth-century colonial New England from angles that have been typically obscured. Her epic tussles with Boston's finest theological minds homed in on questions that have perennially occupied Christians throughout the history of the church, including the relationship between grace and obedience, and between Scripture and experience as sources of authority.

If it's true that she resisted the mould laid out for women nearly four centuries ago, then it's just as true that she resists easy categorisation today. Some have attempted to cast her as a proto-feminist, but that's hard to square with the way she 'defended herself at her civil trial by arguing that she had never violated the boundaries of women's place in society.'[36] Others have depicted her, with some justification:

> 'alternatively as a visionary prophet of freedom of conscience or as the misguided leader of an insurgent faction; as the victim of either her own overreaching ambition or the oppression of a monolithic Puritan 'orthodoxy'; as an imaginative woman who could not distinguish the voice of God from her own menopausal delusions or as a courageous woman who challenged the gender norms of her day'[37]

One gets the distinct impression that Hutchinson's popularity as a rival source of authority – not just among women, but men too – was as much a source of irritation among the colony's leaders as the theological positions she held. 'Anne Hutchinson was not condemned solely because she was a woman,' writes Lindley, 'but her gender made her actions even more offensive, and the Puritan leadership drew far-reaching conclusions from the incident about women and their place.'[38] This midwife-theologian's legacy includes inadvertently giving birth to what would become known as Harvard

---

36   Ibid., p. 144.
37   Hall, *Anne Hutchinson*, p. 145.
38   Lindley, *You Have Stept Out of Your Place*, p. 5.

College: just a week after she was banished, Boston's anxious authorities decided to establish an educational institution to secure the colony against the threat posed by future Anne Hutchinsons.

Demonized in her own day as 'a dangerous instrument of the Devil raised up by Satan amongst us,' today she's celebrated as a pioneer of the primacy of the individual conscience and a virtual midwife of religious freedom in America. Originally intended as an epithet, Winthrop's verdict could equally be interpreted as an accolade: Anne Hutchinson was 'a woman of haughty and fierce carriage, a nimble wit and active spirit, a very voluble tongue, more bold than a man.'[39]

For Further Reading

Timothy D. Hall, *Anne Hutchinson: Puritan Prophet* (Boston: Longman, 2010).

Eve LaPlante, *American Jezebel* (New York: HarperCollins, 2004),

---

39 LaPlante, *American Jezebel*, p. 3.

Chapter 6: Anne Dutton Calvinistic Controversialist

Ian Maddock

There were no survivors. Crossing the Atlantic during the eighteenth century was often perilous, and the ship had apparently foundered not far from the British coast on its long journey from the American colonies. When he first heard of the vessel's fate while in South Carolina, the celebrity evangelist George Whitefield – himself no stranger to many transatlantic passages – wasted no time writing to console one of those instantly widowed, a Mrs. Anne Dutton. The 'ungrateful news' of the death of her husband and Baptist pastor, Benjamin Dutton, made Whitefield 'almost wish for wings' that he 'might fly' and comfort her. He went on, 'How your worldly circumstances are I know not. I can only say that if our Lord brings me to England next year, you shall be heartily welcome to live with me. My Dear Yokefellow [that is, Elizabeth, Whitefield's wife of six years] joins most cordially in this invitation. I hope you will accept of it.'[1] Who was Anne Dutton? As the glue, humanly speaking, that held together the evangelical revival, Whitefield's circle of friends and acquaintances was enormous; what was so special about his relationship with the Duttons – and Anne especially – that he was willing to extend such an open-ended offer of hospitality to her in particular?

If, when he wrote his consoling letter on 27 October 1747, George Whitefield was one of the most well-known figures throughout the transatlantic world, then his contemporary Anne Dutton is quite possibly one of the most significant female figures in the eighteenth-century revivals you've never heard of. A self-made theologian and self-styled spiritual advisor, she overcame many social and religious barriers in order to indisputably become one of the most prolific female writers of her day. Along with a number of hymns, she authored an array of theological treatises and letter-books. She was a correspondent with – and trusted ally of – many key evangelical leaders, including Calvinists like Howell Harris, George Whitefield, William Seward, and Selina Hastings. She was also a spirited critic of others, especially the Arminian John Wesley; a 'Calvinistic controversialist' is how she has since been dubbed.[2]

---

1   Unpublished letter from George Whitefield to Anne Dutton, 27 October 1747.

2   A. Wallington, 'Wesley and Anne Dutton', *Proceedings of the Wesley Historical Society* 11/2 (June 1917), p. 47.

From Northampton, to London, to Great Gransden

Anne Dutton (her maiden name was Williams) was born in 1692 in Northampton, England. She grew up attending a congregationalist church, where she was converted at age thirteen. Two years later she joined the same church as a member. In her autobiography, Dutton describes herself as having a discerning theological mind from an early age. In 1709, her first pastor, John Hunt, died. Anne was not shy about what she felt to be the theological shortcomings of his successor and at the age of seventeen voted with her feet: 'Having received full satisfaction that it was the Lord's mind, I should *remove my communion* from that church to which I was then related, to that over which Mr. *Moore* was pastor. I accordingly did it.'[3]

Her new church was an open-membership Baptist church in Northampton. In the previous century, John Bunyan had vigorously defended this church-governance distinctive that enabled Christians from traditions that baptized infants to become full members of a Baptist church without first being baptized by immersion, so long as they gave credible profession of regeneration. Dutton looked back with great fondness on 'fat green pastures' she enjoyed here: 'The special advantage I received under [John Moore's] ministry, was the establishment of

---

3   Joann Ford Watson (ed.), *Selected Spiritual Writings of Anne Dutton: Eighteenth-Century British-Baptist, Woman Theologian* (Macon: Mercer University Press, 2003), 1:xv.

my judgment in the doctrines of the gospel.'[4] In 1714, Dutton was first married and moved to London with her husband, Thomas Cattell, worshipping together at a Calvinistic Baptist church in Cripplegate. Sadly, their marriage was short-lived, her husband dying five years later in 1719. Widowed for the first time, a grieving Anne moved back to Northampton to live with her family.

She wouldn't remain single for long. Later that year Anne met Benjamin Dutton, a clothier who would eventually become a Baptist pastor, and they married in 1720. Benjamin recollected, 'The first Time I was in her Company with other Friends, I was much taken with her Christian Discourse, and had this Thought pass'd through my Mind, that she would make a brave Minister's wife.'[5] Over a decade would pass before Benjamin's hypothesis would have an opportunity to be tested. During these intervening years – and like his father before him – Benjamin struggled with alcoholism. He recounts this battle – and eventual victory – in his candid autobiography. He also offered comfort to those who despaired that they would ever overcome a besetting sin:

> Say not, 'It will always be thus'. I know Satan will persuade you that it will. But remember, he was a liar

---

4   Watson, *Spiritual Writings of Anne Dutton*, 3:47, 50.

5   Benjamin Dutton, *The Superaboundings of the Exceeding Riches of God's Free-grace, Towards the Chief of the Chief of Sinners Shewn Forth in the Lord's Gracious Dealings with ... Benjamin Dutton* (London: J. Hart, 1743), pp. 128-29.

from the beginning. Watch, pray, strive, and fight still. ...As the God of all grace has forgiven and restored me, be encouraged, O ye dear Children of God who groan under the power of sin, to hope and believe that deliverance will come.[6]

Benjamin Dutton was blessed with godly accountability partners throughout his battle, and when he received a call to pastor a church in Great Gransden in Huntingdonshire, they collectively signed a letter stating that God had granted him 'Repentance and Remission of Sins ... and that he has been enabled to walk for a considerable Time as becometh the Gospel.'[7] Arriving in Great Gransden on 10 October 1732, in many ways Anne and Benjamin proved to be an ambitious couple. Within a year of arriving, Benjamin Dutton had successfully led the process of converting the congregationally governed church from practicing infant baptism to only baptising adult believers. The newly reconstituted church grew dramatically under Benjamin's preaching ministry. By the early 1740s, as many as three hundred people were cramming in and around the small meeting house each Sunday morning.

Defending Her Right to Write

As the congregation grew, so too did Anne's sense of calling to serve the wider people of God through her writing. Writing was more than a hobby – it was

---

6   Ibid., pp. 152-53.

7   Ibid., pp. 102-3.

a 'divine vocation, she believed. God was using her as a kind of amanuensis [that is, a scribe].'[8] As she later put it, Dutton 'possessed an inward inclination, to write and publish many little tracts,' though she readily acknowledged that 'the weakness of my sex' posed an obstacle. Even those who encouraged her literary productivity recognised that she faced an uphill battle gaining a hearing in a time and place where women were not actively encouraged to publish; and if they did, it was often anonymously or else under the guise of a pseudonym. For example, while fellow Calvinist Howell Harris complimented 'the Gentlewoman in the Country' on her theological prowess and hoped she would 'live long to set forth with [her] Pen as publick as possible, the Glory of [God's] Grace,' he nonetheless suspected that her ability to gain a hearing would be difficult in the male-dominated world of eighteenth-century theological debate.[9]

Undeterred – and arguably even emboldened – by the doubters and detractors, Anne proceeded to defend her right to write. In 1743, Dutton published *A Letter to Such of the Servants of Christ Who May Have Any Scruple about the Lawfulness of Printing Anything Written by a Woman*, where she put forward a four-fold defence of her 'ministry of letters.' First, she argued that her 'Design

---

8   S. Stein, 'A Note on Anne Dutton, Eighteenth-Century Evangelical,' *Church History* 44 (1975), p. 487.

9   T. Prince, Jr. (ed.), *The Christian History*. Volume 2 (Boston, 1744-1745) 2:62–64.

in publishing… was only the Glory of God, and the Good of Souls'; in other words, God-aggrandisement, not self-aggrandisement, compelled her.[10] Second, in response to those who suggested that passages like 1 Timothy 2:12 and 1 Corinthians 14:34–35 prohibited her from writing, Dutton argued that the Apostle Paul's multiple injunctions for women to remain silent applied only to 'Publick Authoritative Teaching.' By contrast, '*Printing* is a Thing of a very different Consideration,' akin to 'Writing a private *Letter* to a Friend, or… having private *Conference* with him for his Edification. And this is not only permitted to all the Saints, of whatever Sex they may be.'[11]

And yet Dutton wasn't simply content to assume a defensive or reactive posture. Third, and building on her previous argument, she went on the offensive, contending that far from violating an express biblical prohibition, preventing a woman from privately edifying other Christians was itself a violation of Paul's command in Romans 14:19. Citing this verse – and accentuating its applicability for both men and women – Dutton wrote:

'*Let us therefore follow after the Things which make for Peace, and Things wherewith one* (any one, Male or Female) *may edify another*… And unless *Women* were excluded from being *Members* of Christ's mystical

---

10 Watson, *Spiritual Writings of Anne Dutton,* 3:xlvi.
11 Ibid., 3:xlvi.

Body, *their Usefulness*, in all due Means, ought not to be hindered.'[12]

Fourth, and last, Dutton reaffirmed that in her own mind, her publications fell squarely in the category of private exhortation, which she considered 'the Duty of Women as well as Men.' She pointed to the example of Acts 18:26, where 'we are inform'd that Aquila and Priscilla took unto them, even an eloquent Apollos, a Man mighty in the Scriptures, and Expounded unto him the Way of God more perfectly.' Dutton noted that the only difference between this precedent and her own publications was that the former 'is communicating one's Mind by Speech, in one's *own* private House: The other is doing it by *Writing*, in the private House of *another* Person. Both are still *private*.'[13]

Dutton concluded her letter with a winsome, self-deprecating illustration that simultaneously left no room for doubt about her own sense of the propriety of continuing down the path she'd begun: 'Imagine then, my dear Friends, when my *Books* come to your *Houses* that I am come to give you a *Visit*; (for indeed by them I do) and patiently attend to the Lispings of a *Babe*: Who knows but the Lord may ordain *Strength* out of the Babe's Mouth?'[14]

---

12 Ibid., 3:xlvi-xlvii.

13 Ibid., 3:xlvii.

14 Ibid.

I would have your correspondence enlarged

But beyond her own efforts to justify herself to the broader church, it was her friendship with George Whitefield that did much to legitimise and propel her writing ministry. In the 'Grand Itinerant' Whitefield, Anne couldn't have found a more influential and connected publishing patron. He had read and was greatly moved by one of Dutton's earliest works, *Discourse upon Walking with God*, which she published in 1735. Not long after Whitefield returned from his first trailblazing itinerant preaching tour of the American colonies, in mid 1741 he made a point of visiting the Duttons in Great Gransden. Echoing her husband's initial reaction to meeting Anne more than two decades earlier, Whitefield wrote to a third party, 'I have lately seen her [Dutton]; Her conversation is as weighty as her letters.'[15]

In many ways Dutton and Whitefield were two peas in a pod: 'strikingly similar in temperament and disposition in addition to being of one mind theologically.' They quickly formed a mutually advantageous relationship.[16] He was useful to her. Come the early 1740s and Whitefield was advertising Dutton's tracts in *The Weekly History*, the magazine he'd established to promote revival.

And she was useful to him. Overwhelmed by the sheer volume of correspondence he was receiving and unable

---

15 G. Whitefield, *George Whitefield's Letters, 1734-1742* (Edinburgh: Banner of Truth Trust, 1976), p. 280.

16 Stein, "Anne Dutton," pp. 490-491.

to keep up, Whitefield also began to hand off some of his load to her. In one letter alone he enlisted Dutton to correspond with an eclectic line-up that included the Superintendent of the orphanage he'd established at Bethesda, Georgia, the orphans themselves ('Pray write to my dear little orphans, boys and girls...'), a converted plantation owner, and a Baptist pastor. 'You will excuse this freedom,' instructed Whitefield, in a tone that was in equal measures paternalistic, grateful, and flattering; 'I am willing your usefulness should be as extensive as may be.'[17] This was not a one-off request. A little over a year later, on 13 October 1742, Whitefield wrote, 'You will continue writing to, and praying for, my dear family... I would have your correspondence enlarged, and therefore I set other people writing to you, though I cannot write so much myself.'[18]

They were also peas in a pod when it came to one of, if not the, largest elephant in the eighteenth-century room: slavery. Whitefield owned many slaves in America, and sadly, Dutton didn't do anything to discourage him. In fact, she wrote to Whitefield's slaves on his behalf. Her advice? In her 1743 *Letter to the Negroes,* while she encourages Whitefield's slaves to delight in the spiritual equality and freedom promised by Galatians 3:28, they shouldn't get any ideas about that translating into their physical freedom: '[God] doth not call you hereby from the *Service of your Masters according to the Flesh*; but

---

17 Whitefield, *Letters,* p. 277.
18 Ibid., p. 450.

to *serve him* in *serving them*, in obeying all their lawful commands, and submitting to the *Yoke* his Providence has placed you under.'[19]

She even went on to appropriate Jesus' vicarious sacrifice as an example of obedient suffering for slaves to follow. Appealing to 1 Peter 2:18, she argued that Jesus 'calls you to be meek and patient in Sufferings; and has given you himself for an Example of suffering Afflictions, and of Patience.'[20] If Dutton was an agent of the gospel, then in this area at least, she was no less an agent of the British Empire's reliance upon, and perpetuation of, chattel slavery – and a challenge for us to consider the blind spots in our own lives.

As the scope of Whitefield's ministry grew, so too did Dutton's by association. Her earliest biographer, J.A. Jones, observed, 'her epistolary correspondence was most extensive throughout England, Scotland, Wales, Holland, America, etc...' before adding a note guaranteed to bring historians everywhere to tears: '... so that after her death several sacks, full of letters, were found, which were all burnt.'[21] Dutton mightn't have been widely travelled, but her correspondence was. She reflected, 'But the Lord that call'd me to feed his Lambs,

---

19 Watson, *Spiritual Writings of Anne Dutton,* 5:373.

20 Ibid., 5:374.

21 Cited in Wallington, "Wesley and Anne Dutton," p. 44.

has extended my Usefulness to many at a great Distance, by Writing, and Printing, far beyond what I thought of.'[22]

Come 1743 and Mr and Mrs Dutton's ministry was on a growth trajectory. The Baptist church at Great Gransden had by now well and truly outgrown its premises, so much so that loans had been taken out in order to finance the construction of both a new meeting house and pastor's home. That same year, Anne was no less productive. She published at a prolific rate, producing no fewer than thirteen separate titles, mostly under the initials A.D. 'She often wrote anonymously,' noted MacHaffie, 'not out of modesty or shame,' but in a religious ecosystem that frowned on women contributing to theological debate, simply 'to make certain that her work was published.'[23] By way of contrast, her husband also published his autobiography that year – no anonymity required!

But on 17 October 1743, Benjamin left behind his wife and growing congregation (they did not have children of their own) and travelled to the American colonies to raise money to cover the costs of the church's building works and – while he was at it – promote his wife's growing list of publications. Although his fundraising and promotional tour was from all accounts a success, he was repeatedly thwarted in his efforts to find passage back

22 A. Dutton, *A Brief Account of the Gracious Dealings of God... by which the Work of Faith was Carried on with Power. Part II* (London: J. Hart, 1743), p. 163.

23 B.J. MacHaffie, *Her Story: Women in Christian Tradition* (Philadelphia: Fortress Press, 1986), p. 85.

to England until 1747, when he eventually set sail for home. Tragically, they never arrived: the ship, including Benjamin and everyone else on board, was lost at sea.

It took some time for the news of her husband's fate to filter through to Anne with certainty. 'Instead of my husband's safe return,' an anguished Dutton reflected:

> I heard of his Death, and that he was cast away on his Passage home, by the foundering of the Ship! How grieving was this to Nature! How trying to my Faith and Hope! The real loss of my dear Yokefellow; the seeming Denial of my earnest Prayers; and the Failure of my Expectation, as to his Return.[24]

In a providential twist, Whitefield – who had done so much to help accelerate Dutton's exposure across the transatlantic world – met with Benjamin just prior to his doomed journey. He wrote to Anne, 'Your husband was the Lord's Servant – no doubt he is at rest. I heard him pray a little before he embarked. Weep not for Him too much, nor for yourself.'[25]

A Spirited Opponent

Widowed a second time, Anne lived out the remaining eighteen years of her life in Great Grandsen where she continued to produce a flurry of theological letter-books. Dutton devoted lots of time writing encouraging letters to her Calvinist compatriots, and they confided in her in

---

24 Watson, *Spiritual Writings of Anne Dutton,* 1:xliv.

25 Unpublished letter from George Whitefield to Anne Dutton, 27 October 1747.

turn. 'It is an ease thus to unbosom one's self to a friend and an instance of my confidence in you,' Whitefield gushed.[26] She also wrote on subjects ranging from the spiritual nourishment that comes through participating in the Lord's Supper to the nature of true biblical faith. 'She was a prolific though elusive writer, credited by one source with nearly 50 distinct publications,' reflected Stein.[27]

Dutton might have been a close associate and confidant of many Calvinist evangelical leaders, but she was 'also the spirited opponent of others.'[28] Just as a teenaged Anne wasn't afraid to issue precocious theological judgments, thirty years later Dutton was quite prepared to adopt an adversarial literary posture when she felt doctrines situated at the core of the gospel were being compromised. For example, some of her most spirited opposition was directed towards Whitefield's one-time mentor at Oxford, the evangelical Arminian John Wesley. Dutton took particular exception to the way Wesley parsed the doctrines of perfection and election.

These were doctrines that were close to Dutton's – and Wesley's – heart. In her autobiography Dutton reflected, 'Now, to know whether I was elected, was my chief concern … I wanted to know these things for my own soul … Yet though attended with many fears, I pressed through all difficulties, and cast myself at the foot of

---

26 Whitefield, *Letters,* p. 250.

27 Stein, "Anne Dutton," p. 485.

28 Stein, "Anne Dutton," p. 485.

free grace in Christ.' She went on: 'I viewed all my sins meeting on Jesus! In the finished work of redemption, I viewed my salvation wrought out; and a perfection of peace, pardon, and glory, came flowing down to me in free grace, through the blood of Christ.'[29]

Perfection, election, and free grace: all feature prominently in the way Dutton recounts her conversion. These doctrines are also at the centre of her heated exchanges with Wesley during the formative years of the evangelical revival. These were cherished theological distinctives for Dutton – no less for Wesley – and go a long way to explaining why both were willing to contend for them so vigorously and publicly. In their estimation, this was no mere quibble over semantics – the very heart of biblical Christianity was at stake.

Perfection as Not Attainable in This Life

How much can we expect to be sanctified in this life? What sort of 'perfection' – if any – can we hope for this side of the grave? These questions were front and centre in a series of letters traded by Dutton and Wesley between 1739 and 1741. The answers they supplied represented two distinct theological streams within the burgeoning evangelical movement: Calvinism (represented here by Dutton, who emphasised the ultimacy of God's

---

29 J.A. Jones, "A Memoir of Mrs. Anne Dutton" in *A Narration of the Wonders of Grace*. By Anne Dutton. A New Edition, revised, with a Preface and Collected Memoir by the Author. By J.A. Jones, Minister of the Gospel, Mitchell Street, London (London: John Bennett, 1833), p. viii.

predestining choice in one's salvation, but not at the expense of genuine human responsibility) and Arminianism (represented by Wesley, who emphasised the ultimacy of our choice in receiving the salvation God has freely offered to all). If Dutton was at all intimidated by Wesley's reputation, it isn't reflected in the exchanges she initiated with the Fellow of Lincoln College, Oxford, who would go on to become the unrivalled leader of the Methodist movement.

Their correspondence remained out of the public sphere until 1743, when Dutton went ahead and published all four of the letters she had written to Wesley in a single volume entitled *Letters to the Reverend Mr. John Wesley against Perfection as Not Attainable in This Life.* The title more than gives away Dutton's Calvinist theological opinions on the subject! Unfortunately, none of Wesley's replies survive, except for excerpts embedded within Dutton's letters. For example, she begins her exchanges with Wesley, 'Reverend Sir, Yours I receiv'd, and can't but apprehend, that absolute Perfection is asserted therein, as attainable, and attained by some in this Life. If you, Sir, or any other, have attained such Christian Liberty,' – and here begins her direct quotation from Wesley's first letter, – 'as to be "Free, not only from Fears and Doubts, but from Deadness, Dulness and Heaviness, Wanderings in Prayer, and from every Motion and Affection which is contrary to the Law of Love" you must needs be Perfect, absolutely so".'[30]

It's worth noting that when she refers to 'absolute Perfection,' Dutton has in mind what she styles elsewhere as 'entire' or 'sinless perfection.' This much is clear in her correspondence with Whitefield during this period. For example, she wrote to him bemoaning the idea that: 'There is such a Thing attainable in this Life, as an entire, sinless Perfection; and much more so, for any to think, that they themselves have attain'd it.'[31] As far as Dutton was concerned, not only was the idea of absolute, or sinless perfection contrary to Scripture, it defied human experience – surely even Wesley's! She wrote: 'Oh, my Brother, I doubt not, there are Swarms of foolish, vain, impertinent, wandring, yea, wicked Thoughts, that arise even in Your Mind, in One Day, if not in One Hour: And if you discern 'em not, 'tis strange. Oh pray for the Spirit, to convince you of Sin more fully.'[32]

Dutton defended the Calvinist position that although a Christian has been freed of the guilt and dominion of sin, indwelling sin remains in our mortal bodies as long as we live. She believed that, as much as she pursued 'a full Conformity to [Christ], both in Holiness and Glory,' this is unattainable 'until Mortality is swallowed up of Life; until I bear the Image of the heavenly, as fully as

---

30 Watson, *Spiritual Writings of Anne Dutton*, 1:6.

31 Ibid., 1:2.

32 Ibid., 1:14.

I have born the Image of the earthly.'[33] Dutton readily admitted that there are 'some moments, when God draws very near our Spirits ... [and] so fills our Thoughts, that he leaves as it were no Room for any Thing else.' And yet as wonderful as these sought-after experiences are, she considered them to be exceptions to the rule: 'Such seasons are extraordinary, and not the constant Experience of the Saints in this Low Land.'[34]

But there was more to Dutton's position than simply affirming our Christian imperfection. Just as Luther described the Christian identity in terms of being *simul iustus et peccator* – simultaneously righteous and a sinner – Dutton saw herself as a 'walking both'/and, spiritually speaking: 'For I must tell you... that though I see myself *in* myself, in this mixed State, to be vastly imperfect; yet I see myself in Christ, to be absolutely perfect. I am, even now, in all Respects, compleat in Him.'[35]

It's important to recognise that although Dutton and Wesley sharply differed when it came to how perfect we can expect to be in this life, their genuine theological differences were at least to some degree exacerbated by terminological misunderstandings. In other words, when they each spoke about perfection, they weren't necessarily talking about the same thing! For example – and contrary to Dutton's characterisation – Wesley was always careful to clarify that '*sinless perfection* is

---

33 Watson, *Spiritual Writings of Anne Dutton,* 1:7.
34 Ibid., 1:14.
35 Ibid., 1:8.

a phrase I never use.'[36] His preferred term? *Christian* perfection, by which he meant the possibility of loving God and neighbour with all of our being. God has given us this doctrinal carrot, Wesley believed, as an incentive for us to keep on pursuing holiness. Without it, Wesley felt we'd fall prey to spiritual laziness. In fact, he was just as aghast at Dutton's stance on perfection as she was of his! Wesley's fear was that Dutton's doctrine of Christian (im)perfection was a recipe for Christian mediocrity and unholiness.

Free Grace or Free Will?

The other doctrine close to Dutton's heart that she felt was threatened by Wesley's evangelical Arminianism was unconditional election. In 1742 Dutton published *A Letter to the Reverend Mr. John Wesley; In vindication of the Doctrines of Absolute, Unconditional Election, Particular Redemption, Special Vocation and Final Perseverance.* As her title promises, it amounts to a spirited defence of the so-called five points of Calvinism: Total Inability, Unconditional Election, Limited Atonement, Irresistible Grace, and the Perseverance of the Saints. It also amounts to an attack on Wesley and his theology. The world of theological debate in the eighteenth century was an often-times rough and tumble affair, and Dutton entered the fray with fighting words, charging Wesley with being 'as great an Enemy to the Freeness and

---

36 T. Jackson, (ed.), *The Works of John Wesley.* Volume 11 (Grand Rapids: Baker, 1979), p. 396.

Sovereignty of Salvation-Grace, if not greater, than ever rose up.'[37]

For Dutton, as for Whitefield before her, unconditional election was a shibboleth of theological orthodoxy. Why? Because both of them felt that if you deny it, you've automatically inserted works-righteousness into the salvation equation. And so, just as in 1740 Whitefield had accused Wesley of 'plainly mak[ing] salvation depend not on God's *free-grace*, but on man's *free will*,'[38] likewise Dutton contended that either salvation depends 'upon *God's absolute Grace without you*' or else 'upon your *own inherent Goodness*; your *own Will*'; she contended that 'All that obtain Salvation, must be saved by God's eternal, free, sovereign Grace, and not by their own Free-Will.'[39]

Notice that, like Whitefield, when she speaks of 'free grace,' Dutton has in mind *God's* freedom: His unconditional freedom to give, and His unconditional freedom to withhold, grace. But notice also that unlike Whitefield, Dutton seems to acknowledge the role of prevenient grace in Wesley's theology – the distinctive Arminian doctrine that teaches that God has supernaturally restored a measure of graciously enabled free-will to every person. For instance, she questions Wesley, 'Are you willing to be saved by Jesus

---

37 Watson, *Spiritual Writings of Anne Dutton*, 1:47.

38 G. Whitefield, *George Whitefield's Journals* (Edinburgh: Banner of Truth Trust, 1960), p. 587.

39 Watson, *Spiritual Writings of Anne Dutton*, 1:48-49.

Christ? How came you by your Willingness? Was it of yourself, or of God? If you say,' – and here she alludes to prevenient grace – "'Of God; he gave me a Power to Will, and so he has given every Man if he'll exert it." I reply: Then your willing to be saved, is of God remotely, but not immediately.'[40]

In other words, her acknowledgement of prevenient grace notwithstanding, in Dutton's reckoning, any hint of synergism – even a divinely enabled synergism like Wesley's that explicitly put theological distance between itself and Semi-Pelagianism – inevitably compromised the freeness of grace. Anne went on:

> It was yourself, by exerting the Power given you of God in common with All, that made yourself to differ from the Disobedient, and makes Salvation yours, while they perish... Then no Thanks to the Sovereign Lord of Heaven and Earth for your Salvation; but to your own Arm, to that abominable Idol, proud SELF.[41]

In Dutton's estimation, this was a zero-sum theological equation. However Wesley chose to parse our freedom – free will, or a supernaturally and graciously *freed* will – its presence *adds* works and thus *subtracts* from God's sovereignty. In her own words: 'If Salvation was of him that willeth, It would be of Works: And by that law, boasting cannot be excluded. A saved Soul would then have no reason to praise God's distinguishing grace

---

40 Ibid., 1:48.
41 Ibid.

in his salvation, but his own distinguishing Mind, that made it his.'[42]

A talent of writing for him

Anne Dutton's was a rare female Calvinist Baptist voice on the eighteenth-century evangelical landscape. This was a reality not lost on her: 'I am fill'd with wonder, while I view, how my Lord prepar'd me for his Service.'[43] As Stein has observed, 'This obscure, talented author defied powerful social conventions in her effort to rise above the backstage role commonly assigned to and accepted by women in the religious world of the eighteenth century.' Indeed, her full life is 'striking evidence of the way one woman managed to exert substantial influence within evangelicalism during its formative period.'[44]

A trusted ally of George Whitefield, she was also a spirited critic of John Wesley. By 1741, their robust dialogue had devolved into a monologue; it seems that Dutton's publications on perfection and election proved to be conversation stoppers. In fact, in his last letter to Dutton, Wesley even seems to have pointedly questioned whether she'd even received the Holy Spirit! Dutton curtly replied, 'In answer to your last query, I am sure by inward immediate Consciousness, that the Three-One God dwelleth in my Soul, as that my Soul inhabiteth my body.'[45]

---

42 Ibid.

43 Dutton, *A Brief Account*, p. 162.

44 Stein, "Anne Dutton," p. 485, p. 491.

45 Watson, *Spiritual Writings of Anne Dutton*, 1:35.

In her later years, Anne struggled with a debilitating illness – most likely throat cancer – and died on 18 November 1765 at the age of seventy-three. Largely sedentary in person, Dutton's influence was in many ways just as transatlantic in reach as the peripatetic Whitefield. In fact, her memorial stone, erected in Great Gransden, captures this tension: 'Anne Dutton... resided 34 years in this parish... spent her life in the cause of God [and] was the author of 25 vol[ume]s of choice letters & 38 smaller works.'[46]

A trailblazing, convention-busting figure in some ways, in others Anne Dutton was thoroughly conventional. This was especially true of her critiques of Wesley's doctrines, where she walked in the footsteps of the contributions made by many of her male Calvinist contemporaries, most notably George Whitefield himself. 'Our Lord has entrusted you with a Talent of writing for him,' complimented Howell Harris.[47] Indeed he did! Dutton has not only left us a rich literary legacy, but also a compelling inspiration for future generations of men and women alike to proactively and creatively seek opportunities to edify God's people, both near and far.

For Further Reading

Joann Ford Watson (ed.), *Selected Spiritual Writings of Anne Dutton: Eighteenth-Century British-Baptist, Woman Theologian* (Macon: Mercer University Press, 2003).

---

46 Ibid., 1:ix.
47 Prince, *Christian History*, 2:64.

Chapter 7: Selina, Countess of Huntingdon
Queen of the Methodists

Ian Maddock

'I thank your Ladyship for the information concerning the Methodist preachers,' replied the Duchess of Buckingham in a letter to a fellow noblewoman – though as she went on, it quickly became apparent that she had little sympathy for their theological convictions: in short, she found them 'repulsive.' Even more repellent was the way they were 'strongly tinctured with impertinence and disrespect towards their superiors, perpetually endeavouring to level all ranks,' and seemed to advocate doing 'away with all distinctions.' The Duchess was particularly affronted by the uncomfortable implications of the doctrine of original sin upon her own sense of innate superiority: 'It is monstrous to be told that you have a heart as sinful as the common wretches that crawl on the earth. This is highly offensive and insulting; and I cannot but wonder that your Ladyship should relish any sentiments so much at variance with high rank and good breeding.'

The certain 'Ladyship' on the receiving end of this candid correspondence was the then thirty-four-year-old Selina Hastings, Countess of Huntingdon. A recent convert at the time, Selina was keenly aware that her privileged status within British high society came with rich gospel responsibilities. In practice, this meant doing her utmost to encourage her peers (in many cases, literal peers!) to join her in listening to famed evangelists like George Whitefield – whom she would later enlist as her personal chaplain – preach the gospel. 'Your Ladyship does me infinite honour by your obliging enquiries after my health,' continued the Duchess of Buckingham. 'I am most happy to accept your kind offer of accompanying me to hear your favourite preacher and shall await your arrival. The Duchess of Queensbury insists on my patronising her on this occasion; consequently she will be an addition to our party.'[1]

The above illustration offers us a glimpse into Selina's giftedness as a winsome and persuasive ambassador for the gospel in rarefied aristocratic circles. Before long, she was renowned for making the most of every opportunity on a national scale. Described by one of her contemporaries as the 'Queen of the Methodists,' her unique contribution to this period lay in investing her considerable resources as a patron of the burgeoning

---

1   A.C.H. Seymour, *The Life and Times of Selina: Countess of Huntingdon* (London: William Edward Painter, 1839), 1:27.

evangelical movement. Her entrepreneurial energy was exceptional, establishing and overseeing a network of Calvinistic Methodists (her so-called 'Connexion'), building chapels and populating them with a cadre of preachers, and establishing a seminary to train future generations of evangelists. 'A tornado and a silver spoon wrapped into one, a 5'6" force of nature and the heiress of old money,'[2] the Countess of Huntingdon stood alongside the Wesley brothers and Whitefield as one of the most visible leaders of the eighteenth-century evangelical revival.

To the manor born (and wed)

Selina Hastings was born on 24 August 1707 at Astwell Manor in Northamptonshire. Although her upbringing was materially privileged (her aristocratic parents owned multiple estates), it was also filled with relational dysfunction. Her father, Washington Shirley, the 2nd Earl Ferrers, and mother Mary (herself the daughter of a Baronet), separated when she was only six years old. Her mother relocated to France with Selina's infant sister, while she and her older sister were raised by their father in England. When Washington died in 1729, Selina not only inherited considerable property and money, but also a fractious legal dispute with her mother. Intellectually curious from a young age, her prolific letter-writing career betrays her relatively limited education:

---

2   J. Rinehart, *Gospel Patrons: People Whose Generosity Changed the World* (Reclaimed Publishing, 2013), p. 58.

Selina's 'spelling remained erratic throughout her life,' writes Cook. Her 'handwriting, the bane of any would-be-biographer, remained almost illegible,' and 'she made little or no attempt to punctuate her letters either into sentences or paragraphs.'[3]

When she was seventeen, Selina moved to Staunton Harold Hall in Leicestershire, where she met – and in 1728 married – Theophilus Hastings, 9th Earl of Huntingdon, who lived at nearby Donington Hall. By early 1732, the couple already had four children (three more would follow in the ensuing years). Pregnancy took a heavy toll on Selina's health and as was the custom, on doctor's orders she was sent to Bath to 'take the waters' as a way of recuperating. From all accounts the whole experience was medicinally underwhelming and socially nauseating: 'the most stupid place I ever yet saw' was her blunt assessment.[4] Her expeditions to the ancient Roman spa city would nonetheless leave a lasting impression on Selina, giving her a particular heart to reach the 'fine Ladies' of Bath with the gospel in the coming years.

During the first decade of her marriage, the Countess of Huntingdon might best be described as religious and philanthropic – but not yet converted. She was a regular churchgoer, and found the sexual immorality and decadence that was so endemic in her circles to be

---

3   F. Cook, *Selina: Countess of Huntingdon* (Edinburgh: Banner of Truth Trust, 2001), p. 7.

4   Cook, *Selina*, pp. 21-22.

galling. 'From time to time,' writes Harding, 'she made significant purchases of Bibles, Prayer Books, and other items, so that it seems she was helping religious activities of some sort.'[5] The financial generosity towards worthy causes that would become such a crucial facet of her legacy was also evident. For instance, when Thomas Coram sought to establish what became known as the Foundling Hospital – a home and school for London's deserted infants – as a mother of young children herself, Selina was one of the first to pledge her financial support.

Her religious principles were strictly Calvinistic

It wasn't until 1739 that Selina experienced spiritual regeneration (the preaching of the Methodist itinerant Benjamin Ingham, who went on to marry her sister-in-law Margaret Hastings, seems to have been especially influential), though unlike the Wesleys and Whitefield, she left no detailed account of her conversion. Initially she joined John Wesley in worshipping at the Moravian congregation at Fetter Lane. Selina would soon join him in rejecting their so-called 'stillness' teaching. This was the idea that people should simply and passively wait upon the Holy Spirit to bring about conversion, rather than actively employing the means of grace God has given us: for example, meeting with God's people, reading the Bible, and participating in the Lord's Supper (which Wesley regarded as a 'converting ordinance').

---

5   A. Harding, *Selina, Countess of Huntingdon* (Peterborough: Epworth, 2007), p. 30.

At this point in her journey, the Countess identified herself with the Wesleys' Arminian brand of evangelicalism, renouncing unconditional predestination and embracing the possibility of entire sanctification. In 1741, she read John Wesley's recently published sermon on 'Christian Perfection' and was completely sold: 'The doctrine contained therein I hope to live and die by; it is absolutely the most complete thing I know.'[6] But there was another major theological tributary that fed into the Methodist stream known as Calvinism – one that embraced unconditional predestination and renounced perfection – and Selina regularly crossed paths with many of its prominent advocates, including Whitefield and the Welsh itinerant Howell Harris.

Whitefield, who had recently engaged in a bruising public theological dispute with the Wesley's – one that would permanently divide the Methodists along Arminian and Calvinist lines – did his utmost to win Selina over. She wasn't persuaded – for now at least. On 19 February 1742 she wrote to the Wesley brothers about a recent lengthy conversation with Whitefield, who had 'held forth above two hours upon the doctrine of election and reprobation… telling withal (or giving me to understand) I was an elect.' She reported that she had pushed back with gusto:

'I told him… I should be such a loser by his way [of] thinking [&] that no consideration that I was yet

---

able to see from anything he had said could have any weight... I told him I was so much happier than he was & that not from anything in myself but on my constant dependence upon Christ, & [trusted him for] an absolute deliverance from sin.

Particularly concerned with her views on perfection, Whitefield is said to have asked, 'pray does your Ladyship live without sin?' Selina responded that she didn't, 'but that there was such a state... & that before we died it was absolutely necessary we should be in it.'[7]

Within a few years, however, Selina had begun to find Whitefield's doctrines more compelling – and Wesley's less so. In the midst of longstanding struggles with indwelling sin and a fragile sense of assurance, she discovered great comfort in God's promise to preserve those He had unconditionally chosen from before the foundation of the world. Whitefield's Calvinistic Tabernacle at Moorfields – not Wesley's Arminian Foundry a quarter of a mile away – became her preferred London congregation. In 1746, Harris wrote to Whitefield (then on his second preaching tour of the American colonies), 'The good Countess of Huntingdon has been there [the Moorfields Tabernacle] frequently, and has been much pleased, I am told... My poor prayers will be daily offered up to the God of all grace to keep her steadfast in the faith and to make her a burning

---

7   Cited in Harding, *Selina*, p. 35.

and a shining light.'[8] From this point onwards, for all of her affection for the Wesley brothers, her theological die was cast in a Whitefieldian mould. 'Her religious principles were strictly Calvinistic,' reflected Aldridge two weeks after her death, 'and the doctrines of grace were the marrow and life of her soul.'[9]

I dread slack hands in the vineyard; we must all up and be doing

The Countess of Huntingdon's convictions about God's exhaustive sovereignty and goodness would be put to the test over the course of her life. Of the seven children she bore, Selina would bury six, four of them in infancy or childhood. Two died of smallpox within a few months of each other while at boarding school. In 1746, she would also bury her husband. Theophilus had struggled with heart troubles for a number of years, but despite the best efforts of his concerned friends, he refused to seek medical advice: 'he cannot hold out long' despaired one friend in a letter to Selina, adding that if it would do any good, they were prepared to come on 'hands and knees could he prevail with [Theophilus] to set in, in earnest for the recovery of his health.'[10]

---

8   L. Tyerman, *The Life of George Whitefield* (London: Hodder and Stoughton, 1877), 2:168.

9   W. Aldridge, *A Funeral Sermon, Occasioned by the Death of the Late Countess Dowager of Huntingdon, 3rd of July, 1791* (London: Henry Teape, 1791), p. 22.

10 Cook, *Selina*, p. 97.

Eventually the Earl relented and travelled to London for treatment. But, just a few days before he departed, he had a premonition of his imminent demise, where 'death in the appearance of a skeleton, stood at the bed's foot; and after standing a while, untucked the bed clothes at the bottom.' In his recounting of this eery dream to his wife the next morning, the skeleton then 'crept up to the top of the bed (under the clothes) and lay between him' and his wife.[11] Selina's letter to her husband a few days after he left for London betrays not only her anxious state of heart and mind, but also her deep affection for her husband: 'I shall long to have some account of how my dear jewel is after his journey,' she wrote. 'I hope you will, my dear creature, if you should find yourself the least ill, will allow it not to be concealed from me, for nothing could in this world make me so thoroughly unhappy,' she continued, before admitting that 'could my dear creature see the agonies of mind that at times I suffer on account both of your mortal and immortal part … it would give you most sensible pain.'[12]

Theophilus' dream proved prophetic. Selina would not write or hear from her husband again; just two weeks after his strange dream, he died of a stroke on 13 October 1746 at their Downing Street residence. The Countess of Huntingdon found herself widowed at the age of thirty-nine and at a crossroads in her life.

---

11 Ibid., p. 98. This incident was recounted to Augustus Toplady in 1776.

12 Ibid., p. 98.

Overwhelmed by grief, for the next four months she was a virtual recluse – and even contemplated withdrawing from society permanently. In early 1747 she consulted Howell Harris 'about which was best, to live retired and give up all, or fill her place.' In what would prove to be a pivotal and influential conversation, Harris 'said the latter I thought was right whilst she felt enabled to be faithful and felt the Lord was with her.'[13] Selina was persuaded and from this point onwards, her mind was set: 'I dread slack hands in the vineyard,' she wrote to the congregational pastor Phillip Doddridge; 'We must all up and be doing.'[14]

The hour is coming when some of the mighty and noble shall be called

In many ways, Whitefield – not Selina – was the obvious candidate for the role of 'leader' of the Calvinistic Methodists. Arguably one of the most famous personalities of the eighteenth century, he was the first evangelical celebrity preacher and the public face of the revivals that were sweeping the transatlantic world. But first and foremost, Whitefield was an itinerant evangelist at heart, not an administrator. He had an allergic reaction to anything that threatened to restrict his mobility; he had no interest whatsoever in being tied down by the responsibility of overseeing societies. In his own mind,

---

13 T. Beynon (ed.), *Howell Harris's Visits to London* (Aberystwyth: Cambrian News Press, 1960), p. 137.

14 Seymour, *Countess*, 1:79.

sowing the seed of God's Word was his calling: the task of watering it was for others. He once said, 'Everyone hath his proper gift. Field preaching is my plan. In this I am carried as on eagles' wings.'[15] Contrasting his own ministry with Wesley's, Whitefield wrote to his former mentor: 'My attachment to America will not permit me to abide very long in England; consequently, I should but weave a Penelope's web, if I formed societies; and if I should form them, I have not proper assistants to take care of them.' He continued, 'I intend therefore to go about preaching the gospel to every creature. You, I suppose, are for settling societies everywhere.'[16]

On 5 July 1748, Whitefield returned to England after a four-year stint in America. He was welcomed back ashore by Harris, who immediately whisked him away to meet with Selina at her London home in Chelsea. As a peeress (or member of the British nobility), Selina was entitled to appoint a number of personal chaplains, and she had Whitefield, 'the Prince of Pulpit Orators,' in her sights as just the larger-than-life personality to reach her contemporaries. Over the summer she hosted a series of events to road-test Whitefield's preaching before audiences including, amongst others, Lord Bolingbroke and the former Chief Secretary of State, the Earl of

---

15 Quoted in R. Philip, *The Life and Times of the Reverend George Whitefield, M.A.* (Edinburgh: Banner of Truth, 2007), p. 385.

16 J. Gillies, *The Works of George Whitefield* (Edinburgh: Kincaid and Bell, 1771), 2:169-170.

Chesterfield. They embodied Selina's target audience: rich, famous – and unconverted.

'The Grand Itinerant's' preaching was a hit. Bolingbroke's verdict was that 'Whitefield is the most extraordinary man of our times. He has the most commanding eloquence I have ever heard in any person.' Chesterfield was no less enthusiastic: 'Mr. Whitefield's eloquence is unrivalled – his zeal inexhaustible; and not to admire both would argue a total absence of taste.'[17] Selina was delighted; if anything, her expectations were exceeded. She reported to Doddridge:

> I must tell you that I have had two large assemblies at my house of the mighty, the noble, the wise & the rich to hear the Gospel by Mr Whitefield & I have great pleasure in telling you they all expressed a great deal in hearing of him. Sometimes I do hope for Lord Chesterfield.[18]

Whitefield was no less optimistic after these gatherings: 'I went home never more surprised at any incident in my life. The prospect of doing good to the rich that attend her Ladyship's house is very encouraging. Who knows what God may do?'[19] To one fellow Methodist preacher he wrote, 'The prospect of catching some of the rich in

---

17 Gillies, *Works,* 2:168.

18 G.F. Nuttall, *Calendar of the Correspondence of Philip Doddridge DD (1702-1751)* (London: Historical Manuscripts Commission, 1979), Letter 1392.

19 J. Pollock, *George Whitefield and the Great Awakening* (Garden City, NY: Doubleday, 1972), p. 39.

the gospel net is very promising,'[20] while to his brother James he wondered expectantly if, 'the hour is coming when some of the mighty and noble shall be called.'[21] Even Deists like Benjamin Franklin, who had an intimate working relationship with Whitefield as the main publisher of his Journals and sermons in the American colonies, recognised the tremendous potential societal good that might transpire from the religious awakening of the upper classes. 'If you can gain them to a good and exemplary life,' encouraged Franklin, 'wonderful changes will follow in the manner of the lower ranks.'[22]

Neither Whitefield not the Countess needed any more convincing that they were a perfect ministry match. Soon afterwards Selina offered – and Whitefield accepted – her scarf as her personal chaplain. Always sure to adopt a posture of deference and humility towards his patroness (some have wondered if the cooling relationship between John Wesley and Selina had as much to do with his refusal to acquiesce to her social status as to their undoubted theological differences), Whitefield's unexpected upward social mobility left him giddy with excitement. The son of a publican and a lowly servitor at Oxford University, Whitefield had become, as

---

20 Gillies, *Works*, 2:220.

21 Ibid., 2:170.

22 L.W. Labaree (ed.), *The Papers of Benjamin Franklin* (New Haven: Yale University Press, 1961), 3:383.

he would henceforth always style himself, 'Chaplain to the Right Honourable Countess of Huntingdon.'[23]

Empress of her new connexion

If Whitefield knew himself well enough to realise that presiding over the Calvinistic Methodist societies was not his forte, then the newly appointed chaplain also knew just the person for the job: the Countess of Huntingdon. 'Perhaps the Lord is fitting your Ladyship for some new work,' he wrote in May 1749.[24] Six months later and he was more direct: 'A leader is wanting. This honour hath been put upon your Ladyship by the great head of the church.'[25]

The Countess of Huntingdon assumed the organisational role that Whitefield had declined. Her evangelical entrepreneurialism was 'a critical factor in bringing an evangelical witness to the English aristocracy.'[26] Just as John Wesley established and oversaw a multitude of Methodist Societies (fashioned in his own Arminian theological image and serviced by an array of itinerant evangelical preachers), likewise Selina would establish and oversee societies of her own. Collectively known as 'Lady Huntingdon's Connexion,'

---

23 While an undergraduate he performed menial tasks as the servant of rich students in lieu of the hefty tuition costs that were well out of his family's financial reach.

24 G.M. Roberts (ed.), *Selected Trevecka Letters, 1742-1747 & 1747-1794* (Caernarvon: Calvinistic Methodist Bookroom, 1956 &1962), 2:256.

25 Gillies, *Works*, 2:294.

26 M. Noll, *The Rise of Evangelicalism* (Leicester: IVP, 2004), p. 149.

these were similarly fashioned in her own Calvinistic theological image. If Selina was 'Empress of her new connexion,' suggests Tyerman, then 'Whitefield was her prime minister.'[27] Whitefield's preferred description – that she was more like 'a good archbishop with her chaplains around him' – perhaps better captures her desire to remain a loyal member of the Established church and avoid creating a rival denomination, though this is eventually what transpired in her twilight years.[28]

Beginning in 1750 and extending over the next four decades, 'Lady Huntingdon's preachers' proclaimed the gospel at a constellation of chapels throughout Wales and England. These chapels eventually grew to sixty-four in number, and existed for the express purpose of providing 'places of worship where evangelical men could preach without the strictures often imposed upon them by the hierarchy of the Church.'[29] Her strategy exploited 'the entitlement (whether soundly based in law, or not) for members of the peerage to have a domestic chapel attached to their residence,' notes Harding. He continued, 'Once such a chapel had been established, members of the public could be admitted to its services… whether or not the Countess was actually in residence.'[30]

---

27 L. Tyerman, *The Life of the Rev. George Whitefield* (2nd edition; London: Hodder and Stoughton, 1890), 2:21

28 Cook, *Selina*, p. 154.

29 Ibid., p. 155.

30 Harding, *Selina*, p. 68.

Her initial practice was to lease properties with chapels attached, but in time this made way for building chapels from the ground up. Proximity to water-based leisure and recuperation was a recurring feature of the chosen locations for these chapels, whether it be up-and-coming seaside resort towns like Brighton, or fashionable spa towns like Bath and Tunbridge Wells. 'In Georgian Bath,' a place where Selina had a long history and longed to see transformed by the gospel, she 'chose to employ her favourite style of architecture – the Gothic.' Opened in 1765 with much fanfare, the Bath chapel was created with her target audience's tastes in view: 'With its crenelated frontage, tall arched windows and intersecting tracery,' suggests Cook, 'the chapel was designed as a building in which the aristocratic residents of Bath would feel at ease.'[31] It also had a unique feature: a seat located immediately inside the front door, curtained off from the rest of the sanctuary, where high-ranking Church of England clergy could listen to Selina's preachers incognito! Much of the stigma initially associated with the Methodists wore off as time went on, but as Seymour notes, the prospect of a Bishop 'undergoing the dreadful disgrace of being seen in such a place' meant that 'Nicodemus' Corner' (as it was cheekily dubbed) was often occupied.[32]

The Countess of Huntingdon was careful to schedule public gatherings at times that did not conflict with Church

---

31 Cook, *Selina*, p. 222.
32 Seymour, *Countess*, 1:477.

of England worship services.[33] But in retrospect, conflict – and eventually separation from – the Established church was inevitable. In 1779, just two weeks after she opened her latest chapel at Spa Fields in London, Thomas Haweis – an ordained Church of England clergyman appointed as another of Selina's personal chaplains – had his right to preach challenged in court by the curate of the local parish church. Turnbull notes that '[t]he prosecution case was simple,' and – as it turns out – persuasive. 'A chapel with seating for thousands, a public entrance and tickets sold for seating, could not in any reasonable manner be construed a private chapel.'[34]

The tenuous legal foundation upon which Selina had simultaneously attempted to build her Connexion and remain a loyal member of the Church of England crumbled. The court not only decided against the Countess, but also established a precedent for future ecclesiastical litigation against her chaplains. Faced with the decision to either close her chapels or else register them under the Toleration Act as dissenting meeting houses, in 1782 she reluctantly chose the latter. 'I am to be cast out of the Church for what I have been doing these forty years – speaking and living for Jesus

---

33 E. Welch, *Spiritual Pilgrim: A Reassessment of the Life of the Countess of Huntingdon* (Cardiff: University of Wales Press, 1995), p. 100.

34 R. Turnbull, *Transformed Heart, Transforming Church: The Countess of Huntingdon's Connexion* (London: The Latimer Trust, 2015), p. 16.

Christ,' she lamented, with a dose of defiance.[35] While some of her preachers followed her into dissent, most, like Haweis, remained within the Church of England – and in the process contributed in part to the Calvinistic Methodists failure to flourish to the same degree as Wesley's Arminian Methodist wing.

A true Mother in Israel

The Countess of Huntingdon's chapels multiplied at such a rate that the demand for preachers began to outpace supply. This immediate shortage, coupled in 1768 with Oxford University's decision to expel six students for 'holding Methodistical tenets,' provided Selina with the impetus to challenge Oxford and Cambridge's monopoly on training ministers and establish a 'nursery for preachers' of her own design.[36] Trevecca College (sometimes spelled Trevecka or Trefecca) was the fruit of this vision. Originally a rundown farmhouse near Howell Harris' home in Wales, the Countess single-handedly funded every facet of the College's operations: from its initial renovation and enlargement, to faculty and staff wages, to providing full bursaries for all students. 'In classic evangelical fashion,' her desire was that 'this college would provide for both intellectual equipping, as an alternative to the universities... and be a place for practical preparation for an itinerant preaching

---

35 Cook, *Selina*, p. 375.
36 Harding, *Selina*, p. 87.

ministry.'[37] In addition, she hoped – perhaps naively – that the Church of England would look kindly on Trevecca's graduates when it came to ordination. 'The reality,' observes Turnbull, 'was that only a handful succeeded in this endeavour and the students from the college were treated with much suspicion.'[38]

Trevecca opened on the Countess' sixty-first birthday, 24 August 1768: it was, in effect, a gift from herself to the wider church. Whitefield presided over the opening ceremonies, and in an act of evangelical ecumenism, the Arminian John Fletcher was chosen as the first Principal. By this stage, the Countess of Huntingdon had only two surviving children of her own, and she was estranged from one of them, her eldest daughter Elizabeth. In many ways Trevecca's students would become her spiritual offspring; they certainly saw her in a maternal – if somewhat matriarchal – light. 'She regarded her young men as her sons, as her family,' declared one Trevecca alumni in a sermon preached in Selina's honour soon after her death in 1791. 'With what affection and tenderness, wisdom and prudence, have I heard her address the young men in the study around her. How has she warned, cautioned, reproved, comforted, and encouraged us, as she saw cause, like a true Mother in Israel!'[39]

---

37 Turnbull, *Transformed*, p. 13.
38 Ibid., p. 15.
39 Aldridge, *Funeral Sermon*, p. 18.

In addition to managing her College and navigating the tricky ecclesial waters surrounding her Connexion, Selina's final decades included the challenge of managing another institution, this one from afar: the orphanage that Whitefield had established in Bethesda, Georgia, over forty years earlier. When Whitefield died suddenly in Newburyport, Massachusetts on 30 September 1770, Selina was top of the list of people on the other side of the Atlantic to be informed. The next day, a local minister wrote to her: 'Most Noble Lady, In God's providence an important and sorrowful event took place yesterday, in which I believe your Ladyship to be interested. I mean the death of that truly excellent and faithful servant of Christ, the Reverend Mr. Whitefield.' He continued, 'Being favoured with his acquaintance, I have heard him speak in the highest and most respectful manner of your Ladyship.'[40] His own wife having died a few years earlier – and leaving no heirs of his own – Whitefield bequeathed everything to his patroness, including the orphanage. No doubt intended as a way of honouring her, unfortunately Bethesda proved to be as much of an administrative albatross around her own neck as it did for Whitefield throughout his lifetime – a financial blackhole that never quite lived up to its promise.

---

40 J.R. Tyson and B.S. Schlenther, *In the Midst of Early Methodism: Lady Huntingdon and Her Correspondence* (Lanham: Scarecrow Press, 2006), p. 111.

I wish there was a Lady Huntingdon in every diocese in my kingdom.

If the generosity of wealthy female patrons like Phoebe was integral to the flourishing of the gospel in the first century, then the generosity of wealthy patrons like the Countess of Huntingdon was no less integral to the flourishing of the gospel in the eighteenth century: 'For when I gave myself up to the Lord,' said Selina, 'I likewise devoted to him all my fortune.'[41] The generation of preachers she helped raise up attested to her willingness to lay 'down at the foot of the Cross her honours, titles, distinction and fortune.'[42] 'We are used to aristocrats forming their own regiments or cricket teams,' contends Harding, 'but an aristocrat who started her own *church* is in a class apart.'[43]

Indeed she was! If Wesley and Whitefield are celebrated as 'Founding Fathers' of contemporary evangelicalism, then Selina was no less the movement's 'Founding Mother.' 'The evangelical revival of the eighteenth century might never have gained the acceptance that it did apart from the endeavours of the Countess of Huntingdon,' observed Cook. 'The Countess used her unquestionable influence in the highest circles of the land and even in the royal court to throw the cloak of her protection over the prominent preachers of the day

---

41 Seymour, *Countess,* 1:315.
42 Aldridge, *Funeral Sermon,* p. 24.
43 Harding, *Selina,* p. x.

and over the fledgling Methodist movement itself.'[44] In fact, the verdict from the royal court was nothing short of glowing: 'There is something so noble, so commanding, and withal so engaging about [Selina], that I am quite captivated with her Ladyship,' commented none other than King George III. 'I wish there was a Lady Huntingdon in every diocese in my kingdom.'[45]

For Further Reading

Faith Cook, *Selina: Countess of Huntingdon* (Edinburgh: Banner of Truth Trust, 2001).

Alan Harding, *Selina, Countess of Huntingdon* (Peterborough: Epworth, 2007).

---

44 Cook, *Selina*, p. 128.
45 Seymour, *Countess*, 2:283.

Chapter 8: Catherine Booth
Perfect Equality

RACHEL CIANO

In London, 1885, a thirteen-year-old girl stared down her fate – the fate of so many girls in her situation. Her family was from the poorer classes and, to help make ends meet, her mother sold her for £5 to a procuress of prostitutes: a £3 down payment, and a further £2 once her virginity had been certified.[1] An ex-brothel keeper helped with the exchange, as she knew the trade and had a wealth of contacts in the industry. Once inside the brothel, women took the girl to a room that had been rented for an hour by a man, undressed her, and sedated her with chloroform to prepare her for her ordeal.[2] Afterwards, she was shipped to Paris – the route from London to the Continent was a highway for

---

1   W.T. Stead, 'The Maiden Tribute of Modern Babylon', *Pall Mall Gazette,* 6 July 1885. For excerpts of the article, see also Roy Hattersley, *Blood and Fire: William and Catherine Booth and Their Salvation Army* (New York: Doubleday, 1999), pp. 313–6.

2   Ibid.

child prostitution in the nineteenth century. Despite the commonness of this tale, most British people remained largely ignorant – deliberately or otherwise – of this trade in human lives. Most, but not all. There were exceptions to the apathy-rule, including, amongst others, Catherine Booth. Their involvement in this particular story was to change the course of history.

A delicate constitution

Catherine Mumford was born on 17 January 1829 in Derbyshire, England, born fourth in a family of five children.[3] Both parents were from a Methodist background. The Methodists were a relatively newly established Christian movement based on the teaching and ministry of John Wesley. The Methodist movement's emphasis on all people in society – not just the educated upper classes – hearing and understanding the Bible, as well as its stress on personal holiness, impacted Catherine's later ministry. A year after her death, a contemporary declared, 'the spirit that is embodied in it [the Salvation Army] has come, under God, from the energetic breath of Methodism.'[4]

Her father, John Mumford, was a lay preacher with the Wesleyan Methodists but would eventually part ways

---

3 Tragically, Catherine's three older siblings died as children; only Catherine and her younger brother, John, grew to adulthood. Her brother eventually moved away to America when he was sixteen (Catherine was twenty), and contact appears to have dwindled.

4 John Hugh Morgan, 'Catherine Booth: The Mother of the Salvation Army', *The Wesleyan-Methodist Magazine,* January 1891; 15., p. 14.

with them. In the early 1840s, John became a heavy drinker, and this severely affected his family, especially financially. He would eventually renounce his Christian faith. Catherine's mother, Sarah (née Milward), was earnest about her Methodist faith, and Catherine came to share it too. Sarah educated her daughter at home – a common way to educate girls in nineteenth-century England. Sarah was concerned that her only daughter might be corrupted by a public education (especially learning French and reading novels!) and the influence of children who did not share their faith. Catherine was an avid reader, and by the time she turned twelve, she had read the entire Bible eight times, and had digested the works of John Wesley and the famous nineteenth-century preacher in the American revivals, Charles Finney. These years mainly spent at home were formative for her mind, and the books she devoured fuelled her personal spiritual devotion.

When the family moved to Boston, Lincolnshire, Catherine was allowed to go to school for several years (1841–43) when her mother was convinced by a fellow parishioner that a particular school in the area aligned with her educational philosophy of discipline and serious study. There, Catherine studied broader subjects than she was used to – English writing, mathematics, history, and geography. Unfortunately, she had to stop attending that school when she developed a spinal condition that would leave her bedridden.

Catherine experienced persistent and life-long health challenges, and had what was considered a 'delicate constitution.' She developed a curvature of the spine as a teenager, which made movement difficult and painful; she often spent months at a time confined to her bed. At seventeen, Catherine suffered from consumption (tuberculosis), which – among other things – left sufferers struggling to breathe, severely fatigued, and losing weight. It was one of the most common diseases in the nineteenth century; estimates suggest four million people in England and Wales died of the disease between 1851–1910. Those who survived often struggled with physical repercussions and pain throughout their lives. When Catherine stepped into the public realm, it was despite her pain, not in the absence of it.

The current of our lives must flow together
At Methodist meetings at a local hall in Clapham, Catherine first met William Booth. He would become her life and ministry partner – allies in a shared vision to see England impacted spiritually and physically by the gospel. William was born in 1829, and grew up attending an Anglican church with his parents; his mother was a committed Christian, whilst his father was a nominal one. William also grew up in poverty due to his father's unsuccessful business ventures. After his father's death when William was thirteen, he began regularly attending the Broad Street Wesleyan Chapel. At fifteen, he had a conversion experience whereby

Jesus became real and personal to him. At seventeen, he joined a group of Methodist street preachers and soon led that group, proving a passionate and powerful preacher.

William's twenty-third birthday proved an eventful day for him. First, a wealthy businessman and great encourager of William's preaching ability, Edward Rabbits, offered to financially support him for three months so that he could start devoting himself to preaching full-time. Second, it was the day that Booth recalls, 'I fell over head and ears in love with the precious woman who afterward became my wife.'[5] They had crossed paths several times in the previous months, but this night proved to be a turning point. When he talked with Catherine that night, she was not feeling well. William offered to help her home, and she was immediately impressed by his care, attentiveness, and kindness. Catherine wrote that once he knew she was in 'delicate health' that night, he 'took the situation in at a glance' and sought to help her and make her as comfortable as possible: she remarked that 'his thought for me, although such a stranger, appeared most remarkable.'[6] Writing of the deep and fateful connection they formed that night, she continued:

---

5   Harold Begbie, *The Life of General William Booth*, vol. 1 (New York: Macmillan, 1920), p. 113.

6   Begbie, *William Booth*, pp. 125–6.

We struck in at once in such wonderful harmony of view and aim and feeling on varied matters that passed rapidly before us. It seemed as though we had intimately known and loved each other for years, and suddenly, after some temporary absence, had been brought together again, and before we reached my home we both suspected, nay, we felt as though we had been made for each other, and that henceforth the current of our lives must flow together.[7]

Views so derogatory to my sex

Catherine firmly believed that for their lives to 'flow together,' one key issue she and William must agree on was a view out of step with the culture of their day – the inherent equality of men and women. She would not marry him without this agreement. From early in her life, Catherine Booth believed in the ontological equality of women and men – a moral and intellectual equality based on being or essence. This equality of *being* preceded all of Catherine's future arguments for the equality of ministry roles and tasks.

Catherine's belief in the equality of men and women was profoundly countercultural for her time and place. For example, many leading Victorian thinkers and writers held assumptions about the limited roles and spheres of women, and about their natural intellectual and moral capabilities. John Ruskin (1819–1900), an English writer, philosopher, and social critic, argued for the intellectual inferiority of women, writing in 1864

---

7   Ibid.

that a woman's 'intellect is not for invention or creation, but for sweet ordering, arrangement and decision.'[8] In 1871, Charles Darwin (1809–1882), a poster child of the Victorian era, contended for the moral inferiority of women, attributing this deficit to natural selection. Darwin identified women as more selfless and perceptive, but attributed this to an evolutionary hiccup:

> It is generally admitted that with woman the powers of intuition, or rapid perception, and perhaps of imitation, are more strongly marked than in man; but some, at least, of these faculties are characteristic of the lower races, and therefore of a past and lower state of civilisation.'[9]

In *Wives of England* (1843), dedicated to Queen Victoria, author Sarah Stickney Ellis (1799–1872) wrote of the necessity of women entering marriage to believe

---

8   John Ruskin, *Sesame and Lilies: Two Lectures Delivered at Manchester in 1864* (New York: John Wiley & Son, 1867), p. 90.

9   Charles Darwin, 'The Descent of Man, and Selection in Relation to Sex,' *Evolutionary Writings*. Ed. James A. Secord (Oxford: Oxford University Press, 2010), p. 304. Some evangelicals argued that the traits of selflessness and sacrifice were supremely Christian characteristics, and thus women were spiritually superior. In a speech to women in 1914, Edward Higgins said, '*In the spiritual realm she is capable of accomplishments beyond man, as in the physical realm man is capable beyond woman...her forgetfulness of self and self-interests...has produced a list of heroines (italics original).*' Edward J. Higgins, 'Women as Leaders of the Salvation Army,' *The Officer* 22, 9. (September 1914), p. 587. See also Andrew Mark Eason, *Women in God's Army: Gender and Equality in the Early Salvation Army* (Waterloo, Ontario: Wilfrid Laurier University Press, 2003), pp. 76–7.

in 'the superiority of your husband simply as a man.'[10] She continued: 'It is quite possible you may have more talent, with higher attainments, and you may also have been generally more admired; but this has nothing whatever to do with your position as a woman, which is, and must be, inferior to his as a man.'[11]

In 1853 when Catherine was twenty-four, she heard a sermon from her pastor, Reverend David Thomas. He referred to a woman's 'natural' inferiority in the sermon, emulating the culture of his day. Catherine wrote him an anonymous letter, defending the ontological equality of women.[12] She wrote that she deemed beliefs like her minister espoused that day as 'views so derogatory to my sex, and which I believe to be unscriptural and dishonouring to God.'[13]

The letter gives us insight into Catherine's views as a young woman. She argued at length in this letter for the 'perfect equality' of women and men both intellectually and morally. Her letter was profoundly respectful and acknowledged that she was 'a mental and spiritual

---

10 Ellis, Sarah Stickney, *The Wives of England: Their Relative Duties, Domestic Influence and Social Obligations* (New York: D. Appleton, 1843), p. 24.

11 Ibid, pp. 24–5.

12 The date of the letter is questioned; however 1853 seems the most likely dating. For discussion, see Rodger Green, *Catherine Booth: A Biography of the Cofounder of The Salvation Army* (Grand Rapids, MI: Baker Books, 1996), p. 307n2.

13 Booth Papers, British Library (BL), Add. MS 64806. See also Green, *Catherine Booth*, p. 119.

debtor to your ministry.'[14] However, the letter also packed a punch. She challenged Rev. Thomas to consider the issue of the equality of women carefully:

> Permit me, my dear sir, to ask whether you have ever made the subject of women's equality as a <u>being</u>, the matter of calm investigation and thought? If not, I would with all deference, suggest it as a subject well worth the exercise of your brain, and calculated amply to repay any research you may bestow upon it.[15]

Catherine argued in this letter that a woman's equal intelligence would be inherently clear if women were given the same educational opportunities as men. It was nurture rather than nature, which she believed crippled a woman's intellect.[16] University education for women in England was still a fair way off: Oxford admitted women to degrees in 1920, Cambridge in 1948.[17] Catherine argued that a woman's educational training in England at the time:

---

14 Booth Papers, BL, Add. MS 64806. Rev. David Thomas conducted Catherine's wedding two years later in 1855, so it appears despite the occasion of the letter, she continued in good relationship with him.

15 Emphasis original. Booth Papers, BL, Add. MS 64806. See also Green, *Catherine Booth*, p. 120.

16 For a fuller discussion of Catherine's views here, see Norman H. Murdoch, 'Female Ministry in the Thought and Work of Catherine Booth,' *Church History* 53, no.3 (1984).

17 London University preceded them substantially, admitting women to degrees in 1878.

has hitherto been such as to cramp and paralyse, rather than to develop and strengthen, her energies— and calculated to crush and wither her aspirations after mental greatness rather than to excite and stimulate them....What inducement has been held out to her to cultivate habits of seclusion, meditation, and thought? What sphere has been open to her?[18]

When Catherine came to consider marriage, she was adamant that equality of being within her marriage was of utmost importance. She wanted a husband who shared 'oneness of views and tastes, any idea of lordship or ownership being lost in love. There can be no doubt that Jesus Christ intended, by making love the law of marriage, to restore woman to the position God intended her to occupy.'[19] In a sixteen-page letter to William two months before they married, she reflected on both the joys and frustrations of the church's approach to women:

> Oh, what endears the Christian religion to my heart is what it <u>has</u> done, and <u>is destined</u> to do, for my own sex; and that which excites my indignation beyond anything else is to hear its sacred precepts dragged forward to hear degrading arguments...it is cruel for the <u>Church</u> to foster prejudice so unscriptural,

---

18 Booth Papers, BL, Add. MS 64806. See also Green, *Catherine Booth*, p. 119.

19 Catherine Booth, 'Courtship by Principle,' in *The Highway of Our God* (London: The Salvation Army, n.d.), p. 76. See also Green, *Catherine Booth*, p. 121.

and thus make the path of <u>usefulness</u> the path of untold suffering.[20]

Catherine concluded this letter posing an ultimatum: 'if you gain anything by what I have writ, I should praise God on hearing it, otherwise I do not desire you to <u>answer</u> this.'[21] Answer he did, to his peril. The fallout of his answer led to what William later described as their 'first little lover's quarrel, and the only serious lover's quarrel we ever had.'[22] There was even speculation that it nearly ended their engagement.[23] William conceded that she was correct on the equality of a woman in being, but not of intellect:

> You <u>combat</u> a great deal that I hold as firmly as <u>you</u> do—viz [in other words] her <u>equality</u>, her <u>perfect</u> <u>equality</u>, as a whole—as a <u>being</u>. But as to concede that she is man's <u>equal</u>, or capable of becoming man's equal, in intellectual attainments and prowess—I must say <u>that</u> is contradicted by experience in the world and my honest conviction.[24]

---

20 Emphasis original. The letter is dated 9 April, 1855. They married on 16 June that year. Booth Papers, BL, Add. MS 64802. See also Green, *Catherine Booth*, p. 122.

21 Ibid.

22 William Booth, 'Mrs Booth as a Woman and a Wife,' *All the World* (October 1910), p. 508. See also Green, *Catherine Booth*, p. 123.

23 W.T Stead, *Mrs Booth of the Salvation Army* (London: James Nisbet and Co., 1900), p. 92.

24 Emphasis original. Begbie, *William Booth*, p. 236.

One of William Booth's earliest biographers (his future son-in-law), who was usually completely glowing in his assessment of William, wrote that in this 'serious difference of opinion' he:

> quoted the old aphorism that woman has a fibre more in her heart and a cell less in her brain. Miss Mumford [i.e. Catherine] would not admit this for a moment... indeed she had avowed her determination never to take as her partner in life one who was not prepared to give woman her proper due.[25]

Female Ministry

William and Catherine resolved their disagreement and married in 1855. William held various ministry posts over the next ten years. In 1865, they formed the East London Christian Mission, the precursor to what would eventually become The Salvation Army in 1878. Women were regarded as key to the mission's success in reaching out to the spiritually and physically destitute in society with the gospel. In the 'Orders and Regulations' for the Salvation Army, William stated, 'Women shall have the right to an equal share with men in the work of publishing salvation.'[26] Female involvement in ministry was and continues to be a core trait of the Salvation Army.

---

25 Frederick de Latour Booth-Tucker, *The Life of Catherine Booth: The Mother of The Salvation Army,* vol. 1 (New York: Revell, 1892), pp. 116–7.

26 Mark Galli and Ted Olsen, eds. *131 Christians Everyone Should Know* (Nashville, TN: Broadman and Holman, 2000), p. 299.

Catherine and William were not the first dynamic ministry duo during this period. American Wesleyan Phoebe Palmer (1807–1874) assisted her evangelist husband, Walter, in teaching, which outraged Anglican Minister Arthur Rees. He wrote a pamphlet attacking Phoebe Palmer and denouncing the practice of women preaching. In return, Catherine wrote her lengthy rebuttal, *Female Ministry, or Woman's Right to Preach the Gospel*, in 1859. She defended the idea of the equality of women in ministry. The cover page quoted the prophet Joel: 'And your sons and daughters shall prophesy.'[27] Her central biblical appeal was Galatians 3:28, where the Apostle Paul says, 'There is neither...male nor female, for you are all one in Christ Jesus.' In addition, she argued that the key text for women remaining silent in churches, 1 Corinthians 14:34–35, was not universally applicable outside first-century Corinth and was 'contrary to the example of Jesus.'[28]

As well as arguing from biblical texts, Catherine argued that moral equality allowed women to preach. She drew on the influence of Methodism and John Wesley's emphasis on holiness and the possibility of Christian perfection.[29] Catherine considered the

---

27 Catherine Booth, *Female Ministry, or Woman's Right to Preach the Gospel* (London: Morgan & Chase, n.d.).

28 Henry Gariepy, *Christianity in Action: The International History of the Salvation Army* (Grand Rapids: Eerdmans, 2009), p. 34.

29 Catherine believed, along with Wesley, that justification was salvation from the guilt of sin and restoration to God's favour, and sanctification was salvation from the power of sin and restoration

primary qualification for ministry to be the conduct of a person's life, and because she believed women could attain equal holiness as men, being endowed with the same Holy Spirit, she argued women were therefore equally qualified for ministry. Catherine appealed to women well known for both their holiness and ministry, such as Elizabeth Fry (1780–1845), most famous for her work reforming prison conditions, particularly for women. Catherine argued women like Fry have given 'indisputable evidence by the purity and beauty of their lives that they were led by the Spirit of God.'[30] Given such evidence, she questions how the Holy Spirit who sanctified them could also mislead them concerning their call to ministry.[31] Holiness, the Spirit of God, and female ministry were intertwined and interdependent in Catherine's determination.

Catherine hesitated for several years before preaching, saying she battled 'between the sense of duty and the sense of insufficiency...in an agony of reluctance from stepping outside the usual sphere of womanhood, to bear public testimony for Christ.'[32] Those who heard her preach commented on both her powerful appeal, skilfully combined with a gentle approach. The Archbishop of

---

to the image of God. See Green, *Catherine Booth,* p.192. See also John Wesley's sermon 'On Working Out Our Own Salvation' in Frank Baker, *The Works of John Wesley* (Nashville: Abingdon Press, 1986), 3:204.

30 Catherine Booth, *Female Ministry*, p. 20.

31 Ibid.

32 Morgan, 'Catherine Booth', p.16.

Canterbury's chaplain, Dr Randall Davidson, said on hearing her first ever sermon in 1860, 'If ever I am charged with a crime, don't bother to get any of the great lawyers to defend me; get that woman.'[33] In an era when women were celebrated for their achievements in the domestic rather than the public sphere, Catherine wrote to her mother, 'I feel quite at home on the platform—far more than I do in the kitchen.'[34] When William was ill, she would take his place in the pulpit. Catherine wrote to William, 'I must…do all in the kitchen as well as in the Pulpit to the glory of God.'[35] Time to prepare sermons could be hard to come by, and she wrote, 'I cannot give time to preparation unless I can afford to put my sewing out. It never seems to occur to anybody that I cannot do two things at once.'[36]

It was the best of times?

If Catherine believed in the essential equality of being and inherent value of both men and women, then the same can be said of her beliefs about the equality and value of the lower classes in Victorian Britain. Catherine, along with William, desired people from all social classes to hear the good news of Jesus. The Salvation Army was a direct, gospel-driven response to the difficulties in society they saw all around them.

---

33 Gariepy, *Christianity in Action*, p. 36.

34 C. Booth to parents, 23 Dec 1857, BL, Add. MS 64804, fol. 63.

35 C. Booth to W. Booth [1860], BL, Add. MS 64802, fol. 145.

36 Galli and Olsen, eds., *131 Christians*, p. 299.

Catherine's heart for those in dire need was given ample opportunity to shine, given the conditions of the poor in Victorian Britain. If you have read or seen an adaptation of *Oliver Twist*, *A Christmas Carol*, *Hard Times*, *Tale of Two Cities*, or *Great Expectations*, Charles Dickens (1812–1870) has for better or worse helped shape your imagination of this world. Dickens, who lived and breathed Victorian Britain, made it his mission to highlight the working-class conditions in his novels in order to advocate for change. *Great Expectations*, published in 1860, speaks of the London that Catherine occupied:

> We Britons had at that time particularly settled that it was treasonable to doubt our having and our being the best of everything: otherwise, while I was scared by the immensity of London, I think I might have had some faint doubts whether it was not rather ugly, crooked, narrow, and dirty.[37]

Lower classes in Victorian Britain faced poverty, disease, harsh working conditions, and difficult living situations. Two main factors led to these social challenges; a sharp population rise and the Industrial Revolution. The population of England and Wales more than doubled in the sixty years between 1790 and 1850, from 8.5 million people to 18 million people. It nearly doubled again by the end of the nineteenth century.

---

37   Charles Dickens, *Great Expectations* (London: Penguin, 1996), p. 163.

The Industrial Revolution, which had begun in Britain around 1760 before spreading to Europe and America, brought enormous change to people's lives. New technologies, particularly in manufacturing processes and transportation, completely transformed the physical and social landscape. It was the age of steam power, and the invention of the steam engine transformed society.[38] Steam required continually heating water, which required burning coal in massive quantities, making coal mining a large part of Victorian Britain's landscape. More and more people moved from the country to the city to find work in new factories. The massive influx of people stretched the capabilities of these cities; housing, roads, hospitals, and the police force were all pushed to their limits.

For working class people, working conditions were often horrendous. Factories and mines typically had long hours, dangerous environments, and child labour. Children were cheaper to employ, were fast learners of new technology, and could fit in tight spaces, like mine shafts. They were also small enough to fit under heavy machinery; some scavenged for cotton scraps in cotton factories, which was a very risky task. Until

---

38 Steam engines led to all sorts of new technologies, like the production of iron on a large scale, and new manufacturing machines like textile machines that took over what people used to do by hand. Steam technology also changed how goods, and eventually people, moved around. The steam train and steamboat opened up transport routes, allowing for faster, easier, more affordable travel for raw and finished products, and for people.

the mid-nineteenth century, children were used in coal mines and could work from 4am to 5pm; many died of lung cancer before age twenty-five. Workers in match factories that used white phosphorous could develop 'phossy jaw' which rotted their muscles and bones and often led to a painful death. Prostitution, including of young girls, helped supplement the incomes of poorer households. Alcohol abuse was rampant, and public drunkenness was common among the working classes. The eighteenth-century London gin craze had left its mark, and gin shops – of which there were many in London – sometimes had steps near the counter so children as young as four could climb up and purchase liquor. In time, these social issues were highlighted and eventually acted upon, the Salvation Army being arguably the most significant and influential respondent of this age.

Catherine knew first hand the plight of the poor. She started ministering to alcoholics and their families during William's posting at Gateshead beginning in 1858, and this only grew once The Christian Mission and later the Salvation Army were founded. She deeply felt human need, and her influence on the Salvation Army helped form their stance towards the poor and destitute. The Army conducted a whole variety of ministries, and as they spread internationally, ministries were shaped around local need. For example, they established a match factory in London that used safe, red phosphorous (rather than white) to protect workers from developing 'phossy jaw,' a halfway home in Melbourne, Australia, to assist released prisoners re-entering society; and an institution for recovering female alcoholics in Toronto, Canada.[39] The social justice concern of the Salvation Army was borne out of both William and Catherine's deep desire to see complete transformation of individual people as well as society; for them it was a natural outworking of Christian discipleship and holiness, and an important entry point to preaching the gospel.

The Consent of A Child
Whilst Catherine cared deeply about all people struggling in society, it was particularly prostitutes that captured her heart. Prostitution, particularly forced prostitution and child prostitution, was rife. Young girls, some as young as nine or ten, were sold by their impoverished parents to help ease financial burdens.[40] The Salvation Army encountered prostitutes at Army meetings and on the streets; however, organised attempts to alleviate prostitution only began in 1881. The impetus was a young country girl who attended an Army meeting, who said she had come to London and been lured to a brothel via a false address. Determined not to send her back there, a Salvation Army Sergeant, Mrs Cottrill, took her back to her home, and reasoned that if there was one girl in this situation, there were bound to be more. She kept making room in her house for women

---

39 Green, *Catherine Booth*, p. 248.
40 Roy Hattersley, *Blood and Fire: William and Catherine Booth and Their Salvation Army* (New York: Doubleday, 1999), p. 307.

until alternative accommodation could be found. A safe house was rented in Hanbury Street in 1884 to help with this work, and Catherine's daughter-in-law, Florence Booth, was placed in charge. Catherine took a keen interest in this project and helped furnish the house. This was the beginning of Catherine's interest in the plight of prostitutes in Victorian Britain.

To combat child prostitution and trafficking, Catherine determinedly campaigned to legally raise the age of consent for girls.[41] Prior to 1875 in England, the age of consent for girls was twelve.[42] In 1875, it was raised to thirteen. Unsatisfied with this, Catherine and her allies conducted a nationwide campaign from 1883 to 1885, called the *Maiden Tribute Campaign*. Between 1875 and 1885 a bill recommending raising the age of consent was passed by the House of Lords but failed to make it through the House of Commons three times. One Member of Parliament argued that it should be lowered to ten, incurring Catherine's irate condemnation! She furiously wrote that this MP 'pleaded that it was hard for a man–HARD–for a man–having a charge brought against him, not to be able to plead the consent of a child like that...I could not have believed that in this

---

41 The age of consent was defined as 'the age up to which it shall be an offence to have or to attempt to have carnal knowledge of, or to indecently assault a girl.' See Frederick Coutts, *Bread for My Neighbour: The Social Influence of William Booth* (London: Hodder and Stoughton, 1987), p. 47.

42 The first age of consent in England was set at twelve in 1275 in the Statute of Westminster I.

country such a discussion amongst so-called gentlemen could have taken place.'[43]

Three of Catherine's key allies in this campaign were Josephine Butler, who had long been fighting against the trafficking of girls from England to Continental Europe; W.T. Stead, a prominent journalist, and close friend and early biographer of both William and Catherine; and Bramwell, their oldest son, who was informed by his wife, Florence, of what she encountered in her daily work at Hanbury Street.[44] Together, they formed a formidable team, and engaged in fairly risky behaviour to try and bring this issue out into the open, for sexual ethics were not up for discussion in nineteenth-century Britain.

We previewed this group's most controversial act in the story at the beginning of this chapter; it was entirely staged, and appears to be the first case of investigative journalism. Catherine's consortium, as well as her connections at the safe house in Hanbury Street, came together to produce this highly orchestrated buy. The girl they 'procured' was thirteen-year-old Eliza Armstrong. Both Eliza and her mother were completely unaware of the scheme. The man who rented the room in the brothel

---

43 Emphasis original. Catherine Booth, *The Iniquity of State Regulated Vice*, published in London in 1884. British Museum Catalogue 3275-AA2 (26) 6 (4), 10–11 (typed copy only).

44 W.T. Stead tragically died on the Titanic. One of the last people to see him alive reported he acted selflessly in helping people into rafts, refusing to get in himself, before the freezing water overtook him and he sunk to his death. See Victor Pierce Jones, *Saint or Sensationalist? The Story of W.T. Stead* (East Wittering, West Sussex: Gooday Publishers, 1988), p. 81.

was the journalist who exposed the story – W.T. Stead. He wanted to prove how easy it was to purchase a young girl, initiate her into a brothel, and then traffic her to the Continent. During his time with her in the room, he did not touch her, and ensured that this was verifiable. Along the way, Salvation Army women (one an ex-prostitute) posed as actors in the saga to keep Eliza safe. Once Stead began exposing this to the British public starting on July 6 1884 in his *Pall Mall Gazette*, circulation on the paper went from 12,000 to over 1,000,000 – viral by nineteenth-century standards.[45] Henceforth, it became known as the *Maiden Tribute Campaign*, and Britain could no longer ignore the issue.

In the aftermath of this series of newspaper articles exposing the trade in young girls, Catherine wrote to Queen Victoria at least three times. Catherine pleaded with the Queen to intervene in what she argued was an issue that particularly affected the poor. However, this proved unsuccessful – the Queen may have been personally sympathetic, but didn't want to get entangled in what she saw as a political issue. This avenue closed, Catherine took to prominent platforms such as St James' Hall and Exeter Hall, speaking powerfully and arguing again that this was a human rights issue, particularly of the poor, and that both men and women should be equally protected in the eyes of the law.

---

45   Jones, *Saint or Sensationalist*, p. 26.

Catherine and William petitioned Parliament on the matter, and they received 393,000 signatures in seventeen days. The petition was two miles long – it took eight cadets to carry it into Parliament. The signatories asked for the age of consent to be raised to eighteen, for the procurement of young people for sex to be made a criminal offence with severe penalties, for the right to search brothels for underage girls, or women being detained against their will, and for equality of men and women before the law.[46] Their efforts were eventually rewarded, though not without cost. In 1885 the legal age for girls was raised to sixteen. The victory celebrations would be short-lived. In what appears to be a retaliatory manoevre, those involved in the Eliza Armstrong saga were arrested, including Catherine's son Bramwell, and some jailed, such as Stead. This arose because it was claimed they had abducted Eliza from her father, Charles Armstrong, because only Eliza's mother had consented to sell her. A decade later Charles Armstrong was proven not to be Eliza's father, but the damage was already done.[47] This national crusade cost Catherine physically and mentally and was her last battle to reform Britain.

---

46   It was illegal for a woman to solicit a man for sex, and the petition asked that it should be equally criminal for a man to do so to a woman. For a copy of the petition, see 'The Salvation Army's Petition to the Government,' *The War Cry* (July 26, 1885), p. 1. Also available in Green, *Catherine Booth*, p. 259.

47   For a full account of the trial and aftermath, see Green, *Catherine Booth*, p. 260–6.

A few years later she was diagnosed with a terminal illness, within five years, she would be dead.

A lover of human-kind

Catherine Booth died of breast cancer in 1890, aged sixty-one, survived by William and their eight children. She left an immense legacy in her wake, demonstrated by the twenty-four thousand people who came together for her funeral, and the people lining up to pay her tribute.[48] A few months after her death, an Anglican minister Reverend John Hugh Morgan commemorated Catherine in *The Wesleyan-Methodist Magazine*, writing that 'in an age unparalleled for remarkable women she occupies a front rank.'[49] He summed up the driving spirit of her life: 'in the truest sense she was a lover of human-kind…no difference of circumstance or race made any difference to her. If she had deeper sympathies it was where the need was greatest.'[50] In this way she emulated her Lord and Saviour and 'was baptised richly with the Christ-like spirit.'[51]

As a contemporary familiar with Catherine and her impact, Reverend Morgan's reflections on lessons that can be learnt from her life are helpful for us to reflect on. First, she taught 'that Christian service must have its

---

48 Morgan, 'Catherine Booth', p. 14.
49 Ibid.
50 Ibid., p. 17.
51 Ibid.

basis in Christian character.'[52] Catherine helps remind us that a person's character – publicly and privately demonstrated – is foundational to Christian service. To neglect this is to undermine the very ministry a person is involved in. 'A good voice, a kindly manner' will be helpful secondary traits, but 'the history of Christian work through the ages shows that the chief factor in doing good is a pure and devout Christian character.'[53] Second, Catherine teaches us that 'Christian women are designed to be effective agents in the evangelisation of the world.'[54] Third, Catherine teaches us 'that Christian service never assumes a nobler form than when it seeks the welfare of the low and lost.'[55] She 'recognised with sorrow the tremendous odds against which the multitudes have to fight in the battle of life' and the 'glorious message of pardon and strength which the Gospel rings forth.'[56] May we, too, have a heart full of compassion for those in need of justice, hope and restoration, and seek to care physically and spiritually for those God has fearfully and wonderfully made.

Finally, in Catherine's day, as is the case today, Christians hold a range of views on the place and role of women in ministry. Catherine's stress on the ontological equality of men and women because they equally possess

---

52 Ibid., p.14.
53 Ibid., p.15.
54 Ibid., p.15–6.
55 Ibid., p.17.
56 Ibid.

God's Spirit is an encouragement and challenge to us. In the context of often highly-charged conversations surrounding how women might appropriately express their ministry giftings, Catherine offers us a re-orientation by encouraging us to step back and see the big picture, that all people are made in the image of God. By focussing our attention on the fact that believers share equally in Christ, possess His Spirit, and partake in His kingdom, Catherine encourages us to recognise the image of God in one another, despite differing opinions on the issue. May such an encouragement help us to be men and women who are full of grace and truth as we serve the Lord together.

For further reading

Rodger Green, *Catherine Booth: A Biography of the Cofounder of The Salvation Army* (Grand Rapids, MI: Baker Books, 1996).

Pamela J. Walker, *Pulling the Devil's Kingdom Down: The Salvation Army in Victorian Britain* (Berkley, CA: University of California Press, 2001).

Chapter 9: Gladys Aylward Ai-weh-de – The Virtuous One

RACHEL CIANO

The Undefeated

In 1949, a few lines in a newspaper reported that Gladys Aylward, a missionary in China for nearly two decades, had returned home to England. Her story may well have remained lost in history. However, when BBC journalist and writer Alan Burgess read of her return, it piqued his interest as he was writing and producing a dramatised series of true stories for BBC radio. In this era, families gathered around the radio to listen to features like this (black and white television sets had become more common in households after the Second World War, but colour TV would not feature until the mid-1960s). Burgess was trying to find stories for his project, called 'The Undefeated,' and had a hunch that a woman returning from nearly twenty years in China might have a fitting one. Burgess went to Aylward's home in London, keen to discover if his intuition was correct. He recounted his surprising, somewhat comical conversation with Gladys that day in her sitting room.

The dialogue, in many ways, sums up Gladys' life and spirit – her understated, humble persona is juxtaposed with courage, tenacity, and ingenuity. Burgess explained his purpose, upon which Gladys shook her head very seriously, and said that she was quite certain nothing had happened to her which would be significant enough to warrant a radio play. 'But surely,' he said, 'in twenty years in China you must have had many strange experiences?' 'Oh yes,' said Gladys, 'but I'm sure people wouldn't be interested in them. Nothing very exciting happened.' It was at least fifteen minutes more before she confessed that she had 'once taken some children across the mountains.'

The rest of the conversation went in this manner, and Alan committed it word for word to his memory:

> I explained my purpose, and Gladys shook her head very seriously, and said that she was quite certain nothing had happened to her which could possibly make a radio play.
> 'But surely,' I said, 'in twenty years in China you must have had many strange experiences?'
> 'Oh yes,' said Gladys, 'but I'm sure people wouldn't be interested in them. Nothing very exciting happened.'
> It was at least fifteen minutes more before she confessed that she had 'once taken some children across the mountains.'
> The rest of the conversation went in this manner, a verbatim memory which I have never forgotten:

'Across the mountains? Where was this?'
'In Shanxi in north China; we travelled from Yangcheng across the mountains to Xi'an.'
'I see. How long did it take you?'
'Oh, about a month.'
'Did you have any money?'
'Oh no, we didn't have any money.'
'I see. What about food? How did you get that?'
'The Mandarin [a Chinese leader] gave us two basketfuls of grain, but we soon ate that up.'
'I see. How many children did you say there were?'
'Nearly a hundred.'

I became conscious that I was saying, 'I see,' rather often, and actually I was not 'seeing' anything at all, except that I was on the brink of a most tremendous story.[1]

Alan Burgess had indeed uncovered a remarkable woman with a remarkable story to tell. It is one full of adventure, hardship, faith, persistence, heartache, and even espionage. Across nearly seventy eventful years, her journeys took her from England to China (through Europe and Japan), back to England, and then finally to Taiwan, where she died and is buried. Throughout her story, it is her gospel-empowered resilience and her Christ-shaped humility that comes to the fore. She was a woman who took every opportunity to share the gospel with whomever came her way, and epitomised Jesus' words to be 'as wise as serpents and as innocent

---

1 Alan Burgess, *The Small Woman* (London: Pan Books, 1957), pp. 247–8. Place names updated here and throughout chapter.

as doves' as she did this. Let us look at the tale of the outwardly unimpressive but inwardly magnetic Gladys Aylward.

Always it was China!

Gladys was born on 24 February 1902 in Edmonton, in London's northeast. Her father, Thomas John Aylward, was a postman and warden at the local Anglican Church, St Aldhelm's. Gladys and her three younger siblings were raised in a genuinely active Christian household run by her mother, Rosina Florence Aylward (née Whiskin). She went to Sunday school when she was young but reflected, 'as I grew older I became impatient with anything to do with religion.'[2] However, one night, for reasons Gladys herself could never explain, she went to a Christian meeting: '[t]here, for the first time, I realised that God had a claim on my life, and I accepted Jesus Christ as my Saviour.'[3]

Gladys read an article about China in the Young Life Campaign magazine, which made a big impression on her. She realised that millions of Chinese people had never heard of Jesus and she felt compelled to do something about it. She tried encouraging her friends to go; however, they seemed unconcerned. Finally, after her brother brushed her off by telling her she should go instead of hassling him about going, she began to

---

2   Gladys Aylward with Christine Hunter, *Gladys Aylward: The Little Woman* (Chicago, IL: Moody, 1970), p. 7.

3   Ibid.

think about how this might become a reality. In 1929 she approached, and was accepted for, missionary training by China Inland Mission (CIM). If you have read *10 Dead Guys You Should Know*, this is the mission organisation that Hudson Taylor established in 1865. He did this to help reach the vast interior areas of China with the gospel, for, at that stage, work was primarily confined to the Eastern coast.

Unfortunately, she did not progress as well as was expected in this training. Gladys Aylward had only received a basic education and had begun working as a shop assistant at fourteen, and then as a parlourmaid. She spent three months in CIM's missionary training program. Ultimately, the CIM committee decided that, owing to her limited education, the prospect of her becoming proficient in Chinese was remote, and declined her candidacy. She felt like all her plans were in ruins. Years later, she reflected on this rejection, acknowledging 'how stupid I must have seemed then', and attributed speaking, reading, and writing the Chinese language like a local as 'one of God's great miracles.'[4] Despite her academic failure at the college, Gladys told the committee chairman, 'but I *have* learned to pray, *really* pray as I never did before, and that is something for which I'll always be grateful.'[5] Prayerfulness was to shape Gladys' life and ministry. The committee chairman wondered if Gladys would like to assist two

---

4   Aylward, *The Little Woman*, p. 8.
5   Ibid., p. 9. Italics original.

retired CIM missionaries as a housekeeper, and she took up the offer.

Aylward went to Bristol to help care for Dr and Mrs Fisher and learned much from being with them, particularly by watching their faith and hearing stories of their life abroad. This time was foundational for Gladys: 'their implicit faith in God was a revelation to me. Never before had I met anyone who trusted Him so utterly, so implicitly and so obediently. They knew God as their Friend, not as a Being far away, and they lived with Him every day.'[6] As they told stories of their time on the mission field, they taught her lessons that would shape her in future years as she served overseas. They told her, 'God never lets you down. He sends you, guides you and provides for you. Maybe He doesn't answer your prayers as you want them answered, but He *does* answer them. Remember, no is as much an answer as yes.'[7]

Gladys moved on to work in other areas of ministry, including helping women and girls trapped in or about to be lured into prostitution. Far from abating, the desire to head to China continued to grow in her. In Gladys' mind, 'Always it was China! I could not rid myself of the idea that God wanted me there.'[8] She returned to London and worked as a housemaid to save enough money to afford passage to China. The cheapest fare was by

6   Ibid., p. 9.
7   Ibid.
8   Ibid., p. 10.

train through Europe, Russia, Siberia, and into northern China. The booking clerk advised her against it; the Sino–Japanese War (1931–1945) underway between expansionist Japan and China (with her allies, the Soviet Union, Britain and America) meant she might not get through. However, she continued to make payments on this ticket, and having paid it off in instalments, she then wrestled with the question of where in China she wanted to go.

The answer arrived in the form of Jeannie Lawson, a seventy-three-year-old Scottish widowed missionary, who sought a young person to join her in China to carry on the work she was doing. Gladys Aylward learnt of this and decided that the young person she sought was her. She wrote to Lawson, who replied, 'I will meet you in Tianjin [northeast China] if you can find your way out.'[9] Gladys now had a destination. With the blessing and provision of her parents and friends, she began to pack. Reflecting later on the cost it was to her parents to say goodbye to her, Gladys wrote:

> How good they were to me, I realise more fully now as I look back. How great was the sacrifice my parents were making in allowing their daughter to go off alone to a place thousands of miles away, knowing full well that in all probability they would never see her again. How much I have to thank them for, that they did not try to hold me back.[10]

9   Ibid., p. 15.
10   Ibid.

Escaping the fowler's net

Friends and family gathered to bid farewell to Aylward on the 9:30 am train at Liverpool Street Station on Saturday, 15 October 1932. Once the train arrived at Harwich on the coast of England, she took a boat across the North Sea to the Netherlands. There began the extended train journey that would take her across Europe and into Asia. She met a couple on the train returning to their home in The Hague, having just attended the Keswick Convention, a prominent Christian gathering in the north of England. Learning of Gladys' journey and desire to share the gospel in China, the woman made a pact with her: 'For as long as I live, every night at nine o'clock I am going to pray for you. I want you to write your name in my Bible, and let me write mine in yours.'[11] The man pressed an English pound note into her hands as they said goodbye. England was long behind her, and Gladys wondered what she would do with the English money she could no longer spend. In due course, that one-pound note would play an instrumental role in saving her life.

The train continued its journey via Warsaw and Moscow towards Harbin in northern China. Seven days into Aylward's journey, on 22 October, she crossed into snow-covered Siberia. The train was filling up with Soviet soldiers heading to battle to assist the Chinese Army. The previous year, on 18 September 1931, the

---

11 Ibid., p. 18.

Japanese began their invasion of Manchuria in northern China, a region which bordered Russia and Mongolia. This marked the beginning of the Sino-Japanese War, which would impact Gladys' travel plans both to China and within China.[12] When the train reached the Manchurian border at the Mongolian frontier, all the soldiers disembarked. Amidst gunfire, Gladys got off the deserted train onto the abandoned, dark platform. She sat on her suitcase, freezing and hungry. Officials told her the train would go no further, so Gladys prayed that God would show her what to do next.

She decided to follow the track back through the deep snow to the previous station, Chita. Along this march, she slept out in the open for a night, the sound of howling wolves in the background. Gladys finally arrived, exhausted, cold, and dishevelled. Soldiers explained the convoluted train route to Harbin, avoiding battle areas. She set off again; along the way, she witnessed men, women, and children chained together to prevent their escape, weeping as they were driven along to forced labour camps in Siberia. Gladys never forgot this: 'From that moment I hated Communism with all my being.'[13]

She stopped in Vladivostok, where she had her passport removed from her. Russians wanted to keep her

---

12 Other historians date the beginning of the war as 1937, when China's National Revolutionary Army fired on the Imperial Japanese Army in July at the Marco Polo Bridge in Beijing. For discussion, see S. C. M. Paine, *The Wars for Asia, 1911–1949* (Cambridge: Cambridge University Press, 2012), pp. 123–5.

13 Aylward, *The Little Woman,* p. 26.

there to work on the new machinery; they had changed her profession in her passport from 'missionary' to 'machinist.' She was trapped and only managed to escape with a warning and the help of some locals, at significant risk to themselves. Her only escape was a Japanese boat about to depart, but Russian soldiers seized her and pulled her back on the gangway. She pulled out her one-pound British note for them, and they loosened their grip enough for her to jump onto the boat as it began to move. Gladys likened this to escaping the net of the fowler.

Now on a Japanese vessel bound for Japan, she needed to cross to China from there. On 10 November, after a month of travelling, Gladys arrived in the country she had longed for. Mrs Lawson's assistant, Mr Lu, met Gladys in Tianjin to escort her on the final leg of the journey. After a further train, bus, and two-day mule ride, she finally reached Lawson in Yangcheng, a beautiful town in a valley set between soaring, rugged mountains. Despite having come so far at such a physical and emotional cost, Mrs Lawson's greeting was muted, which Gladys attributed to her Scottish heritage! Gladys later said of her:

> Never were two people more unlike thrown together in a strange land. Jeannie Lawson was old, dour and dogmatic, while I was young, full of enthusiasm and also had a strong mind of my own. There was only one thing we had in common, and that was the firm

belief that God had sent us to this place and had some special work for us to do.[14]

The house was decrepit and filled with falling masonry and rubbish, and Mrs Lawson rented it dirt-cheap because locals believed it was haunted. She was trying to clean it up, but it was a big task, and she could only do a little at once. Gladys asked where she could sleep. Mrs Lawson told her to pick one of the many rooms that opened off the central courtyard. Gladys chose a room, swept the rubbish aside, and asked Mrs Lawson where she could get changed, seeing as there were no curtains or glass in the windows, nor door in the doorway. Mrs Lawson told her, 'Oh, I wouldn't bother to undress. It is so much safer to keep all your things on in bed, then they cannot be stolen.'[15] It was lucky Gladys slept in her clothes; when she awoke the following morning, it was to a sea of peering faces – word had got around that a foreigner had arrived.

Wise as serpents, innocent as doves
Mrs Lawson's plan was to turn the premises into an inn for travellers, called *The Inn of Eight Happinesses*. Mules were necessary to traverse the rough mountain terrain; a 'mule highway' ran through Yangcheng. Muleteers (drivers of mule trains) needed a rudimentary place to stay for the night and some basic food. Gladys had stayed at inns

---

14 Aylward, *The Little Woman,* p. 41.
15 Ibid., p. 37.

like this herself on her journey and knew how rough and uncomfortable they could be. News soon spread through the muleteers of northern China that 'the inn of the foreign ladies is clean, the food was good, and at night they had long stories free of charge.'[16] These were stories from the Bible, told by Mrs Lawson and Mr Lu. Despite the dire predictions of CIM, Gladys picked up the local language and learned some of these stories by heart. At the end of the following year, in 1933, Mrs Lawson became seriously ill and died soon after. Gladys was alone, struggling to have enough money to feed herself, and the only European in that part of China. Gladys prayed anxiously and wondered what would come next.

Gladys came to embody Jesus' instruction to His disciples that as they are sent out with the gospel, they should be as wise as serpents and as innocent as doves (Matt. 10:16). One day at the compound, Gladys received an imposing visitor. He was the local magistrate responsible for law and order in his district. Accompanied by three soldiers, he was dressed in finery with a long, curved sword at his side. He had come for her help. He informed her that the new government had recently outlawed foot-binding, and he would be held personally responsible for stamping it out in his area. Tiny feet in a woman were considered beautiful, and foot-binding was an ancient Chinese custom where a girl's feet were excruciatingly folded underneath themselves and then

---

16 Ibid., p. 40.

bound. As a result, walking was extremely painful and challenging. Despite only being 4'10" tall (147 cm) and having size 3 feet, Gladys' 'large' feet were an object of fascination in this area, and locals would lift up the bottom of her skirt to marvel at them.

The magistrate informed Gladys that as a woman with 'big feet,' he needed her help to inspect women's feet in his jurisdiction because a man was not allowed to do so, and every other woman in the district had her feet bound. He would provide basic food, a meagre wage, a mule, and two soldiers to accompany her – it ticked all the boxes except one for Gladys. She told him that she had come to China to tell people about the God she worshipped. She took a risk and told him, 'If I inspect the women's feet, I shall use the opportunity to preach in all the lonely villages.'[17] He replied, 'I understand and acquiesce. A man's gods are his own affair; I have no religious bias. Also, from the standpoint of this government decree, your teaching is good, because if a woman becomes a Christian, she no longer binds her feet.'[18] Her ability to spot a gospel-opening was shrewd and innocent, a serpent-dove approach.

Gladys divided her time between managing the inn and her foot-binding inspection job. Mr Lu and the elderly cook, Yang, looked after the inn in her absence. Yang volunteered to be a storyteller whilst Gladys was away.

---

17 Ibid., p. 45.
18 Ibid.

His story repertoire was sometimes a creative mash-up; Noah fed five thousand with loaves and fishes whilst sailing his Ark down the coast of Galilee, and Jesus sailed in the Ark with all His animals over the floodwaters to Bethlehem![19] Upon entering a town, the soldiers would summon everyone into the town centre. They announced that 'Ai-weh-de' (the closest approximation in Chinese to 'Aylward') was here as the government foot inspector, that every woman and child must present themselves, and that fathers would be imprisoned if their children had bound feet. 'Ai-weh-de' meant 'virtuous woman,' so it was a fitting name for Gladys Aylward as she embarked on this unique ministry. She did this for work for years and became known as 'The Storyteller.' Reflecting on this period of her life, it is clear she was a woman who prayerfully spotted and acted on opportunities that came her way. She wrote:

> As I look back, I am amazed at the way God opened up the opportunities for service. I had longed to go to China, but never in my wildest dreams had I imagined that God would overrule in such a way that I would be given entrance into every village home; have authority to banish a cruel, horrible custom; have government protection; and be paid to preach the gospel of Jesus Christ as I inspected feet![20]

---

19 Keith Stevens, 'Gladys Aylward (1902–1970) with the Muleteers of Shanxi and Spying for the Chinese,' *Journal of the Royal Asiatic Society Hong Kong Branch*, Vol. 44 (2004), p. 120.

20 Aylward, *The Little Woman*, p. 47.

Northern China now felt like her home. She dressed, ate, spoke, and even began to think like a local. She considered this her country and her people, so she applied to become a citizen. In 1936 she was granted citizenship and took 'Ai-weh-de' as her official name.

Gathering orphans

Although her ministry was varied and fruitful, her life in China was not without challenges. Gladys Aylward struggled with loneliness, isolation, and the husband and children she probably wouldn't have. Utterly depressed one day, she desperately prayed that God would send someone to help her. That day, while returning from a village inspection to report to the local ruler, Gladys noticed a woman sitting with a young girl by the side of the road. Gladys could tell that this little girl was close to death, and she approached the woman to see what she could do. The girl was enslaved and the woman did not care if she lived or died. Sensing an opportunity to make some money from a girl who would likely be dead in a couple of hours, the woman offered to sell her to Gladys. Still, Gladys only had five meagre Chinese coins, the equivalent of ninepence in English money (approximately £2 today).

Gladys took the girl home and cared for her, where she recovered and thrived. Gladys called her 'Ninepence', and said she helped 'fill the aching void.'[21] Soon this girl brought in a young boy from the streets, who in

---

21 Ibid., p. 51

turn invited another two. Eventually, Gladys had about twenty children in her care. Now, she said, 'I could not complain of being lonely. Indeed, often I craved a few moments of peace.'[22] It would not be the end of her loneliness, but she knew God's presence with her. In 1944, she wrote in the margin of her Chinese Bible: 'Lonely! The very word can start the tears…Who walk with Christ can never walk alone. Alone, but not alone. He is here.'[23]

Gladys continued to accumulate children into her care. She discovered some when conducting her foot-binding inspections; children as young as four were enslaved, their feet bound. Others came to her as a result of the ongoing conflict. In 1938, her village became a war zone as Chinese and Japanese troops battled to control her region. Gladys was cut off from communicating via post with her English friends and family; it would be 1941 before she learnt of war there too. Yangcheng kept changing hands – first, the Chinese Nationalist Army, then the Japanese Imperialist Army would gain control. Each time there was fighting, villagers would flee to the hills until the hostilities temporarily ceased. Each time they returned it was to less and less; buildings were destroyed, and what was left was looted. The inn became too damaged to live in, but Gladys used the courtyard as a makeshift field hospital, although

---

22 Ibid.
23 Phyllis Thompson, *A London Sparrow: The story of Gladys Aylward – the small woman* (London: Pan Books, 1972), p. 109.

medical supplies were dismally low. She began living in a nearby house, whose occupants were killed in the fighting. During the war, she kept having children thrust upon her. As the years of fighting went on and on, that number grew to over one hundred. She taught them, fed them, and spoke to them about God.

Over the Mountains

One day, a Chinese General told Gladys of orphanages run with government assistance by Madame Chiang. She was the wife of Chinese Nationalist Chiang Kai-shek, military chief and the leader of the Republic of China from 1928.[24] Madame Chiang was renowned for her social welfare, which included setting up facilities for 'warphans' (as she termed them) – orphans of the Sino-Japanese War. Gladys wrote to her, and Madame Chiang replied that she could help care for these orphans in Glady's care. However, this was on the proviso that Gladys bring the children to Shanxi in unoccupied 'Free China', outside the conflict zone. Shanxi was about 350 kilometres north of Yangcheng, across the mountains. Madame Chiang also offered money for Gladys' work if she or someone else could collect it, so Mr Lu set off on the journey with about a hundred children.

---

24 Chiang Kai-shek continued in this role until his death in 1975, but from 1949 onwards ruled in exile from Taiwan rather than mainland China after his forces were defeated by Mao Zedong. He continued to claim that he was the head of the legitimate Chinese government.

After Mr Lu and the children set out, the situation became perilous for Gladys. She discovered that the Japanese had placed a £100 bounty on her head, dead or alive. She was wanted for giving information to the Chinese about Japanese troop activities as they pushed further into China, gathered from her time inspecting villages. She recalled that 'I often gave information of enemy movements. I suppose I was a spy, but I was Chinese and the Japanese were our enemies. They had despoiled our country, disturbed our way of life and killed our friends.'[25] Having learned of the bounty, she decided to leave Yangcheng, but she found herself surrounded by Japanese troops. Amidst a sea of bullets that tore around her, she escaped across a stream and through a field. After travelling for two days, she was finally united with the group of children. Mr Lu had been arrested as a suspected Japanese spy because his dialect was from an occupied region of China. He would eventually be released, but Gladys would need to transport the children in his place.

Gladys set off on the mountainous mule track to Shanxi with one hundred children aged between three and sixteen. The journey was a gruelling one. They slept by the side of the road or in temples, packed together for warmth, for they had no blankets. Their shoes completely wore out, and they were constantly tired, sore, and extremely hungry. The older children helped carry the

25 Aylward, *The Little Woman*, pp. 68–9.

smaller ones on their backs at times. At the beginning of the journey, a local mayor gave them enough food to get to the next town and two men to carry it. However, this soon ran out, and in each town, they had to beg for food and assistance. Food was scarce in the passing villages: the war had made conditions challenging for everyone. In abandoned towns where there were no villagers, she resorted to asking soldiers for food. However, the armies were retreating in the face of expected Japanese forces, and so they did not have much food to spare. Soldiers warned her that Japanese planes would fire upon them if they were spotted.

They reached the wide expanse of the Yellow River, but there were no ferries to carry them because they had stopped running. Gladys and the children desperately prayed for a solution. Finally, the answer came in the form of a Chinese officer who summoned a boat. Once on the other side of the river, the villagers took them into their homes and fed them – they had not eaten in days. It was a sweet relief after so many moments of fearing they would not make it this far. The children boasted to their new hosts:

> All of us bigger ones helped to carry the little ones, and Ai-weh-de was always carrying one or two of the sick ones. And when we got to the river we waited and waited for a boat. We prayed for the river to be opened so that we could walk across like the children of Israel did, across the Red Sea, but God knew we

were tired of walking so He sent a boat, and that was far better.[26]

They rested in the town for two days before taking a train as far as it would go, before reaching a Japanese-occupied area. Again on foot, they trekked across steep, rocky mountains so high the clouds obscured them, accompanied by two soldiers, without which many children would not have survived. After two days of walking, they spotted a railway station, but soldiers told them train travel was too dangerous. However, one option presented itself – a coal train travelling through in the dark just before dawn. The children would need to remain silent because the Japanese had shot at the train enough already, and hearing voices meant they would undoubtedly attack. The younger children slept heavily that night due to exhaustion, so the older children carried them silently on board, hiding them amongst big chunks of coal. Amazingly they made it through safely. When the young ones woke, it was to screams of laughter that their skin had turned coal-black overnight! Another three-day hike brought them to the locked gates of Xi'an – they would admit no refugees. Someone finally took pity on distraught Gladys and told her where she could find another orphanage, a day's train journey away.

After nearly a month on the road, Gladys' body started to shut down, she noticed that 'by now I was too

---

26 Ibid., p. 94.

ill to remember much of what happened.'[27] She got the children to safety at the orphanage but recalled little else. The next she knew, she was in a hospital back in Xi'an with fever, typhus, pneumonia, malnutrition, and exhaustion. Doctors expected her to die. She lay in hospital for a month, unable to speak and unaware of her surroundings. Finally, Mr Lu found her; he had been set free and was searching for her and the children. He only knew her as Ai-weh-de, but he could help identify her via a book she had given to a boy who accompanied her on the journey; it was an English book with the inscription, 'To Gladys from Aunt Bessie.'[28]

The following two years were somewhat muddled in Aylward's memory, which she attributed to her feeble health. When she had partially recovered, she continued her evangelism and worked amongst lepers. When the Chinese Revolution began in 1949, she returned to England after seventeen years in China. The Revolution wanted outside, foreign influence eradicated from China, which included missionaries. Gladys was never to return to mainland China. In 1957 she settled in Taipei, Taiwan, as head of an orphanage. Other than travelling for speaking engagements, Gladys spent the last twelve years of her life there. She died on 1 January 1970 after a few hours of flu-like illness, and was buried the following day in the hilltop garden of Christ's College, Tamsui (Danshui), facing mainland

---

27 Ibid., p. 99.
28 Ibid., p. 101.

China. Above her marble tomb is engraved her Chinese name, Ai-weh-de, in Chinese characters, along with a small, simple, black-and-white photo of her. Next to this is a short inscription about her life in both English and Chinese. It concludes, 'Unless a grain of wheat falls into the earth and dies, it remains alone; but if it dies, it bears much fruit. John 12:24.'

Humble resilience

Gladys Aylward became a household name to many, much to her consternation. Alan Burgess went on to dramatise her story for the BBC, and in 1957 published her story under the title, *The Small Woman*. It became a best seller and was later turned into a film – *The Inn of Sixth Happiness* – starring Ingrid Bergman, a famous Hollywood actress who, in terms of appearance, could not have been more unlike the character of Gladys she was cast to portray. Ever a self-deprecating figure, Gladys was incensed by the movie and its creative licence with her life. However, the film was a hit, and it helped seal Gladys' popularity. Despite her epic adventures amidst trying circumstances and a fraught geo-political landscape, Gladys still maintained there was nothing particularly interesting about her tale! Burgess helps us understand the woman he met that fateful day when he uncovered her narrative. After that conversation in her London loungeroom, he wrote:

'It was not mock modesty on the part of Gladys Aylward; the stories she had been telling were, to her, the greatest in the world taken straight from the pages of the New Testament; that her own adventures might be worth setting down, she had simply not considered.'[29]

For Gladys, the stories of Jesus that she told to the muleteers, orphans, and townspeople on her foot-binding inspections were marvellous, and everything else paled in comparison. Her adventures seemed to her entirely unremarkable when seen in the shadow of the One in whose name she was doing these things. In this way, she models for us Christ-shaped humility.

Gladys also models for us gospel-empowered resilience. She depended on Christ for the strength to serve Him. Resilience is often measured by how able a person is to pick themselves up again after a setback, and Gladys epitomised this quality. CIM refused to send her to China, yet she prayerfully found a contact there to enable her to go. The journey to China itself presented many challenges, yet she pressed on at each obstacle. Troubles in China and crossing the mountains still saw her continuing on in ministry each day. This was not a self-resilience, a 'white-knuckling' approach to the challenges of life. Rather, it was in dependent trust and reliance on Christ that she was able to continue on, not always sure of the path ahead of her, but certain of the One who walked along with her every step of the way.

At the end of his book, Alan Burgess remarked, 'I thank Miss Gladys Aylward for telling me her story,

---

29 Burgess, *The Small Woman*, p. 248.

and for allowing me to set it down. I can only hope that I have done this small woman justice.'[30] In writing her account here, I hope I have done the same.

For further reading

Gladys Aylward with Christine Hunter, *Gladys Aylward: The Little Woman* (Chicago: IL, Moody, 1970).

Alan Burgess, *The Small Woman* (London: Pan Books, 1957).

---

30 Burgess, p. 249.

Chapter 10: Corrie ten Boom
A Time for War and
a Time for Peace

IAN MADDOCK

The Nazis burst through the front door just after dawn. Raids on homes suspected of harbouring Jews were often timed to catch people in the middle of meals, or else when they were in bed in the middle of the night, but this one came during the early morning hours of 28 February 1944. The watchmaking business and its accompanying residence had been under surveillance for some time. Now the Netherlands' occupiers had evidence to act on their hunch that a Dutch family was secretly protecting Jews, and the Germans sprang into action.

Up on the third floor, fifty-one year old Corrie ten Boom was in bed struggling with a fever when the alarm – installed as an early warning device for any secret guests to take immediate cover – began to buzz. This was no drill. One by one those who were currently taking refuge with the ten Booms – four Jews and two underground workers – rushed upstairs and into Corrie's room and hurriedly crawled through a narrow opening in the closet into 'the hiding place': a tiny, narrow, custom-built room within a room hidden behind a false wall.

And just in the nick of time! The plain-clothed secret police and uniformed soldiers quickly pushed past Corrie's older sister Betsie and elderly father, Casper, and before long had navigated their way through the labyrinthine house and up to Corrie's bedroom, situated at the top far corner of the tall, narrow building. As the Nazis took to the walls with hammers in a furious attempt to uncover the whereabouts of the hideout, a Gestapo agent repeatedly struck Corrie, shouting, 'so you're the ringleader, where are the Jews?' and 'where is your secret room?'[1] Little did he know – nor did the Germans ever discover – that they were hiding not more than five feet from where he stood.

Despite being on the verge of losing consciousness, Corrie refused to give up the whereabouts of their precious houseguests. Neither did any of her family. Frustrated, the Nazis arrested Casper, Betsie, Corrie, and three other relatives. Within ten days, Corrie's father would be dead; and before the end of the year, so too would her beloved sister. The ten Booms' years of faith-driven clandestine resistance were over. But for Corrie, these and other traumatic experiences to come would eventually spur a decades-long post-war ministry

---

1   C. ten Boom, *The Hiding Place* (London: Hodder and Stoughton, 2004), p. 124.

that would see her not only proclaiming the freedom we have as forgiven enemies of God, but also the freedom we now have to freely forgive our enemies.

A Time for Everything

Cornelia ten Boom – or Corrie as she was always known – was born on 15 April 1892 in Haarlem, West Holland (about twenty kilometres west of Amsterdam), the youngest of Casper and Cornelia ten Boom's four children. Her father was a second generation watchmaker; the family business on Barteljorisstraat – called the 'Beje' for short – was first opened in 1837. Fondly referred to as 'Haarlem's Grand Old Man,' Corrie's father passed on an artisanal aptitude to his youngest daughter. Not long after his wife's death in 1920, Casper sent Corrie to Switzerland – the international headquarters of the watchmaking craft – and in 1922 she returned as the Netherlands' only licensed woman watchmaker. But if Corrie inherited her father's trade, it seems she didn't inherit his business sense – or lack thereof! 'Not competitors' but instead 'colleagues!' is how Casper once described the other watchmaking shop located a few doors away.[2] Instead, Corrie's eye for detail extended not just to the intricacies of the watches themselves, but all of the associated financial obligations that came with running a family operated business. As events would

---

2   E. Metaxas, *7 Women and the Secret of Their Greatness* (Nashville: Thomas Nelson, 2015), p. 115.

transpire, her organizational skills and high EQ would be put to a very different use in two decades time.

But above and beyond passing on any talent for repairing timepieces, as Christians and members of the Dutch Reformed Church, Casper and Cornelia's greatest longing was to nurture their children in the truth of the gospel. Corrie had an active faith from a very young age, and grew up in a household where showing compassion for the outcast, despised, and marginalised was an integral part of what it meant to be a member of the ten Boom family.

A concern for the spiritual and physical well-being of the Jewish people had been on the hearts of the ten Booms for many generations. In 1844, Corrie's great grandfather Willem began a prayer meeting – held in the Beje – devoted to the salvation of the Jewish people. Looking back after the war, Corrie reflected on how God answered those prayers: 'It was in the same house, exactly one hundred years later, that Grandfather's son, my father, and four of his grandchildren, and one great-grandson were arrested for helping save the lives of Jews during the German occupation of Holland.'[3]

They also had a deep concern for the spiritual and physical well-being of the defeated and destitute. In the months following the end of World War One, the ten Boom's accommodated four malnourished German children whose parents were unable to provide for them

---

3   C. ten Boom, *In My Father's House: The Years Before 'The Hiding Place'* (London: Hodder and Stoughton, 1975), p. 13.

in the immediate aftermath of the war. Throughout the 1930s, they also hosted – and in effect functioned as a surrogate family for – a number of children of Dutch missionaries serving in Indonesia. Far from being an imposition, the ten Booms were energised at their arrival: 'Our quiet, thin little three-storey house was suddenly stretching its walls and echoing the activity of three children. The side door swung in and out like a pendulum on one of our clocks, and it was a good sound.'[4]

Within the wider community, the ten Booms' willingness to extend hospitality, whatever the inconvenience and cost, was legendary. 'Our house was not very big, but it had wide open doors,' reflected Corrie, noting that '[m]any lonesome people found a place with us, where there was music, humour, interesting conversations, and always room for one more at the oval dinner table.'[5] When another missionary family learned that the accommodation arrangements they had previously made for their daughter back in the Netherlands had fallen through at the last moment, they telegrammed a sure solution: 'Send her to the Beje. They always have room, but if they don't, they'll make it.'[6]

While Corrie never married or bore any children of her own, she had a profound impact on the lives of many younger than her herself. In 1923, she and Betsie

---

4   Ten Boom, *Father's House*, p. 113.

5   Ibid., pp. 33-34.

6   Ibid., p. 114.

began forming hiking, gymnastics, and music clubs as a way of discipling teenage girls; Corrie even attended international Girl Guides leadership development conferences in Latvia and Austria. Formal religious education typically finished when children were twelve years old in the Netherlands, but the sisters recognised that they could offer a distinctive Christian voice for young people during their critical and often confusing teenage years. The slogan for the gymnastics club aptly captured the spiritual and physical goals of the group: 'We make straight what is crooked.'[7]

Corrie also taught Bible classes in local schools. 'One of those classes was for children who had learning difficulties. It was such a joy to know that the Holy Spirit doesn't need a high IQ in a person in order to reveal Himself,' she recollected, adding that '[e]ven people of normal or superior intelligence need the Lord to understand the spiritual truths which are only spiritually discerned.'[8]

A Time for War
By the late 1930s, the rhythms of life for the ten Boom family were rich, varied, often happily claustrophobic – and lived out in peacetime conditions. But the storm clouds of war had been brewing steadily throughout the latter half of the decade and eventually they burst on 1 September 1939 when Germany invaded Poland.

---

7   Ibid., p. 138.
8   Ibid., p. 124.

In a sign of things to come, the Poles were swiftly overwhelmed by the Wehrmacht's blitzkrieg tactics.

Soon the Nazis turned their attention westward, and on 10 May 1940 they launched their invasion of France, Belgium, Luxembourg – and the Netherlands. The Dutch offered spirited, but short-lived, opposition. On the evening of 14 May, the Luftwaffe dropped 97 000 tonnes of explosives on the nearby city of Rotterdam: 'I sat bolt upright in my bed. What was that?' remembered Corrie. She continued, 'There! There it was again! A brilliant flash followed a second later by an explosion which shook the bed.' Her memories were vivid: 'I scrambled over the covers to the window and leaned out. The patch of sky above the chimney tops glowed orange-red.'[9] Nearly one thousand civilians were killed and roughly another 80 000 were left homeless by the air raid – a chilling example of 'total war' that didn't differentiate between civilian and military targets. Its design and purpose was simple and singular: battering the Dutch into immediate submission.

Whatever hopes the Netherlands had of maintaining the neutrality they had enjoyed in World War One were dashed in the course of that one catastrophic night; they surrendered to the Nazis the very next day. 'I had not cried the night of the invasion,' wrote Corrie, 'but I cried now, for our country was lost. In the morning the radio announced tanks advancing over the border.'[10]

---

9   Ten Boom, *Hiding Place*, p. 62.

10 Ibid., p. 64.

Life changed overnight for the Dutch. Everyone now had to wear an identity card around their necks and present it on demand. Ration cards were the official means of obtaining groceries and, before long, food would be in short supply. Local newspapers suddenly became propaganda organs for the Nazi war machine. Private radios were quickly confiscated: the ten Booms turned in their portable radio but took a big risk and kept their bigger one hidden beneath a staircase so they could keep up with uncensored news via Allied broadcasters. Corrie's youth clubs – such an integral part of her life and the lives of many – were summarily banned. 'The hardest thing to get used to was the German uniform everywhere, German tanks and trucks in the street, German spoken in the shops,' Corrie recalled.[11]

But as changed and challenging as life had become for the ten Booms, it was impossible not to be dismayed at the worsening plight of the Dutch Jews under Nazi rule. The yellow star of David that all Jews were required to wear was clearly intended to function as a badge of shame, not honour – a way of identifying and humiliating Jews at the same time. Corrie's older brother Willem, an ordained pastor, had anticipated the rise of anti-Semitism during his time spent studying theology in Germany during the 1920s. In a letter to his wife he predicted 'that in a few years' time, there will be worse pogroms than ever before. Countless Jews from

---

11 Ibid., p. 65.

the east will come across the border to seek refuge in our country. We must prepare for that situation.'[12] His doctoral thesis was entitled 'The Birth of Modern Racial Anti-Semitism in France and Germany.'

The anti-Semitism that Willem feared would metastasize and take hold in France and Germany also became increasingly visible in the occupied Netherlands. The Dutch were often willing collaborators with their oppressors in enforcing ever-escalating Nazi persecution of the beleaguered Jewish population. Synagogues were burned to the ground. Signs in shop windows read 'Jews will not be served' and 'No Jews.' Before long, there were fewer and fewer bright yellow stars to be seen. 'Worst were the disappearances,' remembered Corrie; 'A watch, repaired and ready, hanging on its hook in the back of the shop, month after month. A house... mysteriously deserted, grass growing in the rose garden... We never knew whether these people had been spirited away by the Gestapo or gone into hiding.'[13] Little could she imagine that by the end of the war, out of 150 000 Dutch Jews, roughly 75 percent would perish in the Holocaust.

A Time to Love
Maintaining anonymity – let alone helping Jews evade the clutches of the Nazis – was extremely difficult given

---

12 C. ten Boom, *Father ten Boom: God's Man* (Old Tappan, NJ: Fleming H. Revell, 1978), p. 107.

13 Ten Boom, *The Hiding Place*, p. 68.

the constant malevolent surveillance. But with their abiding affection for the Jewish people, together with a seemingly limitless capacity for hospitality, the ten Booms had all the raw ingredients for occupying a crucial role in the local resistance movement's efforts to save Jewish citizens. In God's providence, Corrie and her family had been preparing – and been prepared – for this moment their whole lives. She acknowledged as much: 'A person doesn't spring into existence at the age of fifty; there are years of preparation, years of experience, which God uses in ways we may never know till we meet Him face to face.'[14]

In the end, it was more a case of opportunities for resistance finding the ten Booms rather the ten Booms finding opportunities for resistance. Their entrée into this hazardous existence came unexpectantly and unsought in November 1941 when four German soldiers arrived at their Jewish neighbour's store, and dragged Mr Weil, the owner, outside at gunpoint. After leaving him alone on the street while they returned to ransack the premises, Corrie and Betsie whisked him into the Beje before they could think twice about any repercussions. 'We had not planned our rescue work,' Corrie reflected. She added, 'People started coming to us, saying, "The Gestapo is behind us," and we took them in. Soon others followed.'[15]

---

14 Ten Boom, *Father's House*, p. 154.

15 C.C. Carlson, *Corrie ten Boom: Her Life, Her Faith* (Old Tappan, NJ: Fleming H. Revell, 1983), p. 78.

And they began to follow in numbers. 'My name is Kleermaker. I'm a Jew,' announced a frightened woman at their door one night looking for refuge. 'In this household, God's people are always welcome,' responded Casper.[16] News quickly spread of the ten Booms' reputation for kindness to Jews. Two nights later, an elderly Jewish couple arrived on their doorstep and were welcomed in. But how to feed their guests? The success of their efforts depended not only on their own – but others' – willingness to take risks. Corrie approached a friend at the Food Office. Fred Koornstra not only had access to ration cards, but, most importantly, was sympathetic to their cause. At first, when asked how many cards she needed, she intended to say five. But out of her mouth came the number 100! Through Koornstra's bravery and inventiveness (he staged a fake robbery – where he was the 'victim' – in order to get hold of such a large number of ration cards), the ten Booms were able to expand their sphere of influence beyond the scope of Haarlem.

Before long, Corrie found herself at the centre of a complex people-concealing operation that included thirty boys, twenty girls, twenty older men, and ten women.[17] It's estimated that between late 1941 and early 1944 they helped hide more than 700 Jews in the Beje, which functioned as a form of way station. Another six became permanent residents of the Beje. Communications within

16 Carlson, *Corrie ten Boom*, p. 78.
17 Ibid.

the network were necessary – but always fraught. Although they had a friend at the telephone exchange, Corrie developed a system – appropriately configured in the language of watches – for coding their underground messages. 'We have a woman's watch here that needs repairing. But I can't find a mainspring. Do you know who might have one?' meant, 'We have a Jewish woman in need of a hiding place and we can't find one among our regular contacts.' 'I'm sorry, but the child's watch you left with us is not repairable. Do you have the receipt?' meant, 'A Jewish child has died in one of our houses. We need a burial permit.'[18] When a small triangular wooden sign with 'Alpina' (a brand of watch) printed on it was in the shop window, it was safe to bring 'guests' – but not when it wasn't there.

But if it took a virtual village to rescue that many Dutch Jews, in the end it only took one saboteur to bring it to an end. 'We were too big; the group was too large, the web too widespread,' Corrie reflected after the war.

'Ostensibly we were still an elderly watchmaker living with his two spinster daughters above his tiny shop. In actuality the Beje was the center of an underground ring that spread now to the farthest corners of Holland. Here daily came dozens of workers, reports, appeals. Sooner or later we were going to make a mistake.'[19]

---

18 Ten Boom, *The Hiding Place*, p. 98.
19 Ibid., p. 106.

In the end, Corrie's 'mistake' was letting her guard down and offering help to their would-be and soon-to-be betrayer. When a stranger (they would later learn his name was Jan Vogel) turned up unannounced early in the morning of 28 February 1944, Corrie sensed danger. He was completely unknown, came without any references, and, tellingly for Corrie, was unable to look her in the eyes. 'My wife has just been arrested. We've been hiding Jews you see. If she is questioned, all of our lives are in danger,' Vogel said. His request was simple: six hundred guilders in order to bribe the guards and secure his wife's release. 'I'm a poor man – and I've been told you have certain contacts.' Corrie was suspicious and she hesitated. 'And yet how could I risk being wrong?' she remembered thinking. 'Come back in half an hour. I'll have the money,' she said.[20]

Instead, in half an hour it wasn't Vogel who returned to the Beje, but a posse of plain-clothed Gestapo officers and German soldiers. Corrie was dragged downstairs from her third-floor bedroom to join the rest of her family in the first-floor dining room. Quick-thinking Betsie feigned clumsiness and knocked the Alpina sign out of the windowsill so as to ward off any Jews seeking their help – but was aghast to see one of the German soldiers reach down, pick it up, and place it back where it belonged! As a result, many visitors that morning didn't realise the danger and were also caught up in the raid.

---

20 Ibid., p. 121.

Although the Nazis didn't discover the hiding place or its inhabitants ('We'll set a guard around the house till they've turned to mummies' vowed one of the Germans), they did discover both the old radio and a stash of ration cards – both more than sufficient grounds for arrest. If that wasn't bad enough, the phone began ringing off the hook: 'Miss ten Boom, you're in terrible danger!... They know everything! You've got to be careful!'[21] The Gestapo officer heard everything.

Corrie, her sister Betsie, father Casper, older brother Willem, another older sister, Nollie van Woerden, and her twenty-year old son Peter (a talented organist, who had earlier been briefly incarcerated by the Nazis for bravely playing the Dutch national anthem after church one Sunday morning) were all arrested and taken to the local police station. The next day they were transferred to the Gestapo's Dutch headquarters in The Hague, and then immediately afterwards on to the nearby gaol at Scheveningen, where the guards separated the men and women. Their parting was etched on Corrie's memory: 'Father, God be with you!' she cried. 'And with you, my daughters,' he replied.[22] February 29, 1944 would be the last day they ever saw their father alive.

A Time to Mourn

At first Corrie was put in a cell with four other women. Seeing that she was clearly sick with a serious fever,

---

21 Ibid., pp. 126-127.
22 Ibid., p. 134.

the other inmates vacated the sole bed for her use. But on March 16 – and without explanation – she was moved to solitary confinement. Alone in her cell, Corrie gradually recovered from her illness and found evidence of God's kindness in the midst of suffering. She showered for the first time in six weeks, recollecting 'the warm water over my festering skin' and 'the streams of water through my matted hair.' She found company in the form of a 'small busy black ant,' crouching down and admiring 'the marvelous design of legs and body.'[23] Her sole interactions with other humans took the form of interrogations as the Gestapo attempted to uncover the extent of Corrie's network of resistance workers. Even in the middle of these high-stakes inquisitions, Corrie's evangelistic spirit was irrepressible; one officer in particular was struck by the resilience of her faith despite her circumstances.

For one so used to constant congenial company, Corrie's unrelenting isolation was crushing. Snippets of news were like gold dust. On April 20, when the guards left the prisoners unmonitored to celebrate Hitler's 55th – and second to last – birthday, news flowed in torrents between the cells. Some of it was prophetic but untrue: 'The Allies have invaded Europe' (the invasion wouldn't take place for another forty-seven days); 'The war cannot last another three weeks longer!' (the war in Europe was over the following April). Other news was true and

---

23 Ibid., p. 144.

the fulfilment of Corrie's fervent prayers: 'Nollie van Woerden. Released!'; 'Peter van Woerden. Released!'; 'Willem ten Boom. Released!' Tellingly, no one seemed to know the whereabouts of her father, Casper.

One week later, a package arrived from Nollie bearing a light blue sweater, a bright red towel, and some other supplies: 'How Nollie understood the gray color-hunger of prison,' Corrie rejoiced. But even better than the gifts was the hidden message embedded in the brown paper in which they were wrapped. Corrie's eyes were drawn to Nollie's unusually slanted handwriting, pointed at an angle towards the stamp in the top right corner of the package. 'Hadn't a message once come to the Beje under a stamp, penciled in the tiny square beneath?' she wondered. Corrie carefully worked the stamp free, and sure enough, there was the news she had been longing to hear. 'All the watches in your closet are safe': for those with ears to hear, all six people in the hiding place had escaped![24]

Corrie's euphoria was only short-lived. Not long afterwards, on May 3, another letter arrived from Nollie. It began on a foreboding note: 'Corrie, can you be very brave?' If this was the letter Nollie had dreaded writing, it was the one Corrie had long dreaded receiving: 'Father survived his arrest by only ten days. He is now with the Lord…'[25] To help her not to lose track of time, Corrie had etched a record of significant dates on the

---

24 Ibid., p. 146.
25 Ibid., p. 148.

wall of her cell. 'February 28, 1944: Arrest. February 29, 1944: Transport to Scheveningen. March 16, 1944: Beginning of Solitary. April 15, 1944: My Birthday in Prison.' Under these she now added one more date: 'March 9, 1944: Father released.'[26]

A Time to Weep

For Corrie, this was truly one of the most difficult seasons of her life – a time to weep. And nor was it over. When the Allies began their invasion on the beaches of Normandy on June 6, she and her fellow inmates were relocated inland to the Herzogenbusch concentration camp in Vught. Two months later they were on the move again. As the Allies made steady inroads into German-held territory, Corrie, Betsie, and over one thousand female prisoners were crammed tightly into boxcars, deprived of food, water, and any semblance of sanitation, and forced to endure a torturous four day stop-start journey into northern Germany.

Simultaneously stripped of their humanity, she noted that 'like infants, on hands and knees, we crawled to the opening [of the carriage] and lowered ourselves over the side.' This horrendous odyssey was a foretaste of what awaited them at their destination: the notorious Ravensbruck concentration camp for women. Inmates were depersonalised and reduced to numbers: Betsie and Corrie were 'Prisoner 66729' and 'Prisoner 66730', respectively. The guards lived up (or rather, perhaps,

---

26 Ibid., p. 143, p. 148.

down) to their reputation for sadistic brutality; one female guard in particular, known as The Snake, took seeming delight in humiliating prisoners.

Life at Ravensbruck, especially the punishing work schedule, was perversely designed to create, expose, and ultimately destroy any hint of weakness. Corrie remembered how 'Betsie and I had to push a heavy handcart to a railroad siding where we unloaded large metal plates from a boxcar and wheeled them to a receiving gate at the factory. The gruelling workday lasted eleven hours.' And they were better off than some! 'At least, at noontime,' she reflected, 'we were given a boiled potato and some thin soup; those who worked inside the camp had no midday meal.' Their plight was met with abuse from the guards. She recalled that 'the soldiers patrolling us bellowed and cursed, but we could only shuffle forward inches at a step,' along with the way 'the local people turned their eyes another way.'[27]

But in amongst their experience of cruelty at the hands of fellow creatures made in the image of God, there was also evidence of their Creator's blessing. While other prisoners were thoroughly searched and had all of their personal possessions confiscated, Corrie was able to hide her small Bible. The fleas that infested Barracks 28, Corrie and Betsie's 'home,' had the effect of deterring any soldiers from entering, and thus allowed them to run informal worship services without interference.

---

27 Ibid., p. 187.

Overcrowding was a blessing too: all the more people to offer the comfort of the gospel! Throughout their ordeal, Betsie's God-given determination to 'Rejoice always, pray constantly, [and] give thanks in all circumstances' was an inspiration to Corrie: 'There is no pit so deep that he is not deeper still,' Betsie once said. 'Life at Ravensbruck took place on two separate levels, mutually impossible,' remembered Corrie: 'One, the observable, external life, grew every day more horrible. The other, the life we lived with God, grew daily better, truth upon truth, glory upon glory.'[28]

Despite her robust faith, Betsie was always more physically frail and susceptible to illness than her younger sister. Within a month of their arrival at Ravensbruck, her health had severely deteriorated; on 16 December 1944 she finally succumbed. But before Betsie died, she had shared with Corrie a conviction that both of them would be released before New Year's Day. In one sense, Betsie already had experienced emancipation – but what prospect did Corrie have of being released from prison?

Out of the blue, during roll call on the morning of 28 December, the loudspeaker blared Corrie's name: 'Ten Boom, Cornelia.' It had been so long since she had heard her own name that at first she didn't react. But then her mind started racing: 'What was going to happen? Why had I been singled out? Had someone

---

28   Ibid., p. 182.

reported the Bible?' She followed the guard to the administration barracks and joined a queue of other inmates. 'Entlassen!' – released! – declared the officer to the woman two ahead of Corrie. 'Entlassen!' – released! – he announced to the woman immediately in front of her.

Now it was Corrie's turn. 'I stepped to the desk, steadying myself against it,' she remembered. 'The officer, wrote, brought down the stamp, and then I was holding it in my hand: a piece of paper with my name and birthdate on it, and across the top in large black letters: CERTIFICATE OF DISCHARGE.'[29] As Corrie began her long and circuitous journey home through war-torn countryside, many of the women her age at Ravensbruck were soon afterwards gathered and executed. Humanly speaking, her release was most likely the result of a clerical error.

A Time for Peace
After reuniting with Nollie at the Beje, Corrie began the slow and disorienting readjustment to post-incarceration – and in May 1945, post-war – life. She devoted herself to running a rehabilitation centre for concentration camp survivors and proclaiming what it meant to receive – and offer – the forgiveness that we can possess through faith in the merits of Jesus' atoning blood alone. In the first months after the end of the war, Corrie offered a courageous and counter-cultural model of what it looked

---

29   Ibid., pp. 205-206.

like to forgive one's enemies as she opened her home to Dutch citizens who had betrayed their countrymen and women and sided with the Nazis during the German occupation. Corrie 'saw them frequently in the streets... these former collaborators... turned out of homes and apartments, unable to find jobs, hooted at in the streets,' and in an extraordinary reversal, offered them refuge in the Beje.[30]

In the years that followed, Corrie led a largely peripatetic existence. A self-styled 'tramp for the Lord,' she travelled widely on speaking tours that eventually attracted the attention of the famed evangelist Billy Graham, who helped turn her remarkable story into a series of best-selling books.[31] The first of these, *The Hiding Place*, 'is probably the most widely read Holocaust literature in evangelical circles.'[32] She eventually settled in California in 1977, and after a series of strokes, died on her birthday in 1983, aged 91.

Corrie didn't simply preach forgiveness: she practiced it – sometimes with great difficulty and at great cost. After one speaking engagement, 'I saw him...the former S.S. man who had stood guard at the shower room door in the processing center at Ravensbruck. He was the first of our actual jailers that I had seen since that

---

30 Ibid., p. 219.

31 Ten Boom, *Father's House*, p. 154.

32 Y. Ariel, 'The Faithful in a Time of Trial: The Evangelical Understanding of the Holocaust', *Journal of Religion & Society* 3 (2001), p. 2.

time.' Without warning, 'suddenly it was all there – the roomful of mocking men, the heaps of clothing, Betsie's pain-blanched face.'[33]

Since the war's end he had become a Christian. He was a new man – a new creation – and now he was approaching Corrie! 'How grateful I am for your message *Fraulein*,' said her erstwhile persecutor, holding out his hand. 'I tried to smile, I struggled to raise my hand. I could not. I felt nothing, not the slightest spark of warmth or charity,' she recalled. 'And so again I breathed a silent prayer. Jesus, I cannot forgive him. Give me Your forgiveness.' As she shook his hand, God answered her prayer: 'And so I discovered that it is not on our forgiveness any more than on our goodness that the world's healing hinges, but on His. When He tells us to love our enemies, He gives, along with the command, the love itself.'[34]

For Further Reading

Corrie ten Boom, *In My Father's House: The Years Before 'The Hiding Place'* (London: Hodder and Stoughton, 1975).

Corrie ten Boom, *The Hiding Place* (London: Hodder and Stoughton, 2004).

---

33 Ten Boom, *The Hiding Place*, p. 220.
34 Ibid., pp. 220-221.

Also Available from Christian Focus Publications...

10 DEAD GUYS
YOU SHOULD KNOW

STANDING ON THE SHOULDERS OF GIANTS

EDITED BY IAN J. MADDOCK

ISBN 978-1-5271-0608-6

10 Dead Guys You Should Know

Ten fascinating bite–sized biographies of the Christians people expect you to know.

Edited by IAN J. MADDOCK

While Christians have always prized the Bible as our ultimate authority in matters of faith and practice, we also recognize that the Christian life is an intergenerational and communal activity. This collection of ten short biographies will introduce you to Christians from a variety of places and times, who all boldly preached the gospel, despite the risk to personal reputations and safety. How short–sighted it would be not to glean insights from our ancestors, whether that entails learning how to walk in their steps – or else avoiding their missteps.

Written by Ian Maddock, Rachel Ciano and Stuart Colton, who all teach church history and edited by Ian Maddock. Each chapter has suggested further reading, and additional suggestions 'for the adventurous'.

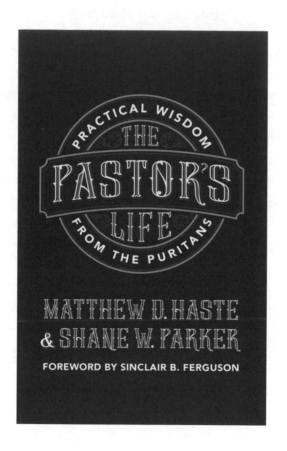

PRACTICAL WISDOM

THE

PASTOR'S

LIFE

FROM THE PURITANS

MATTHEW D. HASTE
& SHANE W. PARKER

FOREWORD BY SINCLAIR B. FERGUSON

ISBN 978-1-5271-0367-2

The Pastor's Life

Practical Wisdom from the Puritans

Matthew D. Haste and Shane W. Parker

The men whose stories appear in this book made up a network of pastors. Through personal contact, or influence, or by reading each other's books, they were bound together in a spiritual brotherhood. They shared a common burden to see God glorified, His Son magnified, and His Spirit honoured by wholesome and practical biblical preaching, wise pastoral counselling, church and family strengthening, and faithful Christian living. Haste and Parker introduce us to these men, their theology, and the lessons we can learn from them.

In this book Matt Haste and Shane Parker have given us the opportunity to gather around the metaphorical table with wise, seasoned pastors, long gone from this visible world. This book can help the reader to think through not just the importance of personal piety and pastoral skill, but also to see examples of how to pursue such things.

Russell D. Moore
Editor in Chief at Christianity Today

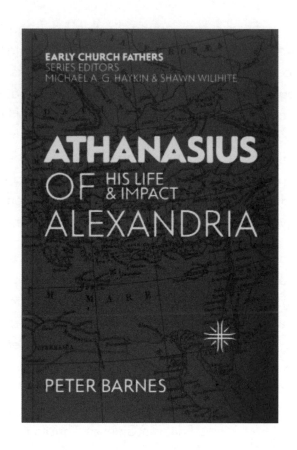

EARLY CHURCH FATHERS
SERIES EDITORS
MICHAEL A. G. HAYKIN & SHAWN WILIHITE

ATHANASIUS
OF HIS LIFE
& IMPACT
ALEXANDRIA

PETER BARNES

ISBN 978-1-5271-0392-4

Athanasius of Alexandria

His Life and Impact

PETER BARNES

From the foreword: Until his death in 373, Athanasius was the most formidable opponent of Arianism in the Roman Empire. Ultimately, for him, this fight was not a struggle for ecclesial power or even for the rightness of his theological position. It was a battle for the souls of men and women. Athanasius rightly knew that upon one's view of Christ hung one's eternal destiny. As he wrote to the bishops of Egypt in 356: 'as therefore the struggle that is now set before us concerns all that we are, either to reject or to keep the faith, let us be zealous and resolve to guard what we have received, bearing in mind the confession that was written down at Nicaea.' And by God's grace, his victory in that struggle has been of enormous blessing to the church ever since.

Athanasius, whose name means 'immortal,' lives on in this comprehensive and commendable biography. Barnes shows how the animated controversialist managed a full life, as a Nicene theologian, Alexandrian bishop, and five-time refugee. The influence of the patriarch persists through these informed pages.

Paul Hartog
Professor of Theology, Faith Baptist Theological Seminary,
Ankeny, Iowa

Christian Focus Publications

Our mission statement –

STAYING FAITHFUL
In dependence upon God we seek to impact the world through literature faithful to His infallible Word, the Bible. Our aim is to ensure that the Lord Jesus Christ is presented as the only hope to obtain forgiveness of sin, live a useful life and look forward to heaven with Him.

Our books are published in four imprints:

CHRISTIAN
FOCUS

Popular works including biographies, commentaries, basic doctrine and Christian living.

CHRISTIAN
HERITAGE

Books representing some of the best material from the rich heritage of the church.

MENTOR

Books written at a level suitable for Bible College and seminary students, pastors, and other serious readers. The imprint includes commentaries, doctrinal studies, examination of current issues and church history.

CF4•K

Children's books for quality Bible teaching and for all age groups: Sunday school curriculum, puzzle and activity books; personal and family devotional titles, biographies and inspirational stories – because you are never too young to know Jesus!

Christian Focus Publications Ltd,
Geanies House, Fearn, Ross-shire,
IV20 1TW, Scotland, United Kingdom.
www.christianfocus.com